Developing
A Data Dictionary
System

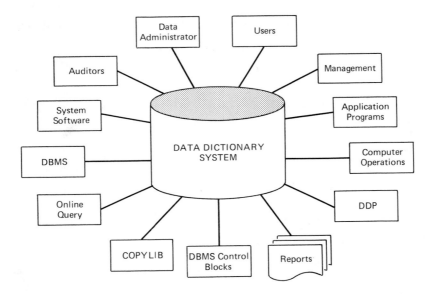

DEVELOPING
A DATA DICTIONARY
SYSTEM

J. VAN DUYN

D. P. Management Consultant
and Adjunct Faculty Member
California State University, Sacramento
School of Business and Computer Science Program

Prentice-Hall, Inc., Englewood Cliffs, NJ 07632

Library of Congress Cataloging in Publication Data

Van Duyn, Julia.
  Developing a data dictionary system.

  Bibliography: p.
  Includes index.
  1. Data base management. 2. Data dictionaries. I. Title.
QA76.9.D3V33   001.64'25   81-7352
ISBN 0-13-204289-4   AACR2

Editorial/production supervision
  and interior design by *Daniela Lodes*
Manufacturing buyer: *Gordon Osbourne*

Printed in the United States of America
10 9 8 7 6 5 4 3 2 1

Prentice-Hall International, Inc., *London*
Prentice-Hall of Australia Pty. Limited, *Sydney*
Prentice-Hall of Canada, Ltd., *Toronto*
Prentice-Hall of India Private Limited, *New Delhi*
Prentice-Hall of Japan, Inc., *Tokyo*
Prentice-Hall of Southeast Asia Pte. Ltd., *Singapore*
Whitehall Books Limited, *Wellington, New Zealand*

CONTENTS

3

WHAT IS A DATA DICTIONARY SYSTEM?   21

4

BENEFITS OF THE DATA DICTIONARY   35

CONTENTS AND FUNCTIONS OF A DATA DICTIONARY SYSTEM 45

STEPS PRIOR TO BUILDING A DATA DICTIONARY SYSTEM 55

7

BUILDING A DATA DICTIONARY SYSTEM 69

8   OVERVIEW OF AN OPERATING DATA
        DICTIONARY SYSTEM   83

11 OVERVIEW OF COMMERCIAL DATA DICTIONARY/DIRECTORY SYSTEM PACKAGES 149

PREFACE

Because data dictionary system concepts and functions (as in the case of data base concepts and functions not too long ago) are far from being understood or appreciated, the objective of this book is to provide a comprehensive, pragmatic source of knowledge about data dictionaries in a direct, easy-to-read language. Moreover, to emphasize its practical approach, sample applications of existing in-house developed and commercially available data dictionaries are included in the text.

Although most of the book deals with the development of in-house data dictionaries, it also gives an overview and survey of the basic features and capabilities of the better known commercial data dictionary/directory software packages for mainframes *and* minis. So that the reader will realize immediate benefits from using the book, it provides a minimum of discussion and a maximum of functional examples and sample applications. Specifically, the first chapter introduces the primary objectives of the data dictionary system (DDS) and discusses briefly the future of this DP tool. The next chapter presents the fundamental difference between file and data base systems, pointing out the sharply different approaches that can be taken to a data base. Chapters 3, 4, and 5 detail the capabilities, benefits, contents, and functions of the different categories of DDS. Chapters 6 and 7 explain the planning and building of a data dictionary. Chapters 8, 9, and 10 give an overview of an operating DDS, a DDS used in systems development, and a DDS in maintenance cycle.

The final chapter displays a comparison chart of the available commercial data dictionary/directory system packages. It also discusses the criteria for selecting a package and provides as a sample one of the better known commercial DD/D system packages: UCC TEN DATA DICTIONARY/MANAGER.

This book is intended for computer systems analysts/designers, Management Information Services (MIS) managers, auditors, data administrators, programmers, and operations supervisors concerned with the planning, design, implementation, and maintenance of a data dictionary system. It is also meant for college students whose curriculum of computer systems and data processing would not be complete without considering the data dictionary system: a concept whose time has come.

ACKNOWLEDGEMENTS

My gratitude to the individuals listed below for their cooperation in providing me with portions of their in-house developed data dictionary systems to be used as examples:

Ho-Nien Liu, Manager
Computer Systems Technology Department
Pacific Gas & Electric Company, San Francisco, CA

W.R. Martin, Assistant Administrator
Data Management and Telecommunications
Veterans Administration, Washington, D.C.

Thomas E. Murray, Manager
Information Services Development
Del Monte Corporation, San Francisco, CA

My appreciation to Thomas E. Milyo, University Computing Company, Dallas, TX, for allowing me to present the UCC TEN Data Dictionary/Manager as an example of a commercially available system.

Has Patel, MSP INC. (Datamanager), Alexander R. DeVito, Synergetics Corporation (Data Catalogue 2), and others were most helpful in giving me the latest data on their commercial data dictionary/directory systems.

And finally, my special thanks to Daniela Lodes, Prentice-Hall, Inc., for her able and conscientious assistance in producing my book.

J. VAN DUYN

Developing
A Data Dictionary
System

1

INTRODUCTION

Whether achieved or not, the objectives of computer systems, from file management systems and centralized data bases to data base management systems and the rapidly emerging distributed data bases, are to establish systems that provide some or all of the following:

1. A reliable system with high utility factor.
2. The ability to share and interchange data among data bases, systems, subsystems, and applications.
3. Data independence.
4. Elimination of nonplanned redundancy.

1

5. The ability to track which programs use particular data.

6. An efficient cataloging method.

7. An automated, well-maintained documentation method.

8. A technique that facilitates updating, restructuring, maintenance, and change control.

9. An efficient query scheme that provides key information to management, preferably on a real-time basis.

To effect these objectives, however, many problems—both technical and human—have to be addressed and solved. Moreover, the increasing complexity of computer systems (especially that of distributed data bases), as well as the growing demand of management for the computer system to justify its cost and to actually support decision making, calls for an integrated tool: a tool that is capable of recording and processing information about the structure and usage of all the enterprise's data and functions; a tool that can be a substantial aid in systems development and maintenance as well as in the handling and controlling of data.

Such a device is the data dictionary system (DDS). A DDS may be structured very simply and contain only the assigned names and numbers, a limited description of data elements, and certain information to document files and programs. A more complex and truly useful DDS, featuring online updating and reporting, may be structured to consist of a set of automated procedures and data for performing the following minimum functions:

1. Generate control definitions needed by the computer system(s).

2. Ensure data independence.

3. Integrate data bases access capability.

4. Analyze transactions.

5. Evaluate system performance.

6. Perform file conversion.

7. Allocate files.

8. Validate data.

9. Stop unauthorized access to unique data and files.

10. Record the frequency and volume of sensitive data and files being accessed.

Note: Regardless of how efficient and sophisticated a data dictionary system is, it does not eliminate the need for good management, clearly defined objectives, and qualified data processing personnel. The well-structured, properly implemented and maintained DDS however does ease the tasks of all users, both programmers and nonprogrammers, and provides systems analysts/designers and data administrators an effective tool for the control and management of corporate data resource.

1.1   WHAT ABOUT THE FUTURE OF DATA DICTIONARIES?

The latest survey in the DP field indicates that the future of this highly useful tool is bright indeed. According to this poll, data dictionaries will have an increasingly important role in the 1980s. To touch upon the main points in this forecasting:

1. The use of DDS will be an accepted part of systems development and maintenance as well as of logical data analysis.

2. The use of DDS among non-DP staff will be much more extensive than at the present time.

3. The DDS will be used to direct and control distributed data bases, and to monitor the security of data base management systems.

2

FUNDAMENTAL DIFFERENCE BETWEEN FILE AND DATA BASE SYSTEMS

Before discussing the what, why, and how of the data dictionary, a clarification of what distinguishes the data base system from the file system is in order.

The basic difference between a conventional file or application system and a data base system is in the philosophy. A file system (whether on cards, tapes, or disks) is designed to receive, store, and produce specific information/output that requires specific input. This approach or philosophy satisfies the requirements of a particular application like payroll, sales, inventory control, and others—each application containing its own distinctive data elements—of a certain department manager. In other words, the file system—even a large-scale Management Information File System—is a collection of individual files of organized records that serves the current information needs of specific applications. (A sample application showing usage of a Management Information File System is presented on pp. 13–16.)

The data base system on the other hand, especially when under the control of a Data Base Management System (DBMS) such as Cincom System's Total, IBM's IMS/VS, Cullinane Corporation's IDMS, and Software AG's Adabas, to mention some of the better known data base management sysems, is much more than a collection of files. It does not store information as information. It stores data to be used in generating multiple levels and types of information. Specifically, a data base is designed to incorporate all the data elements or data resources that mirror the organization's activities—both automated and nonautomated—to meet the information requirements of the whole enterprise in an accurate, controlled, and timely manner. It can share online useful information across organizational lines because it is cognizant of how the work flows from department to department and of the logical interrelationships between departments; it can provide ad hoc reports, and it is directly accessible. Moreover, because each data set contains multiple records or segments, it can give multiple views of the same data and show the relationships among various data. It also has the facility for both physical and logical expansion or changes and, by maintaining data independence, the DBMS can provide high data integrity. A data dictionary system—either standing alone or as part of the DBMS' software—can take over many of the functions above thus enabling the DBMS to concentrate on its primary functions. In addition, a DDS can provide minimal data redundancy and central control that enforces security and standards.

2.1   MAJOR APPROACHES

A discussion of the distinction between application systems and data base systems would not be complete without giving an overview of the different approaches among data base management systems. The three major approaches follow:

1. The hierarchical approach—in which records or segments are organized in a hierarchical or tree-structure manner. A hierarchical DBMS such as System 2000 establishes parent-child-twin relationships by physical juxtaposition of records, or

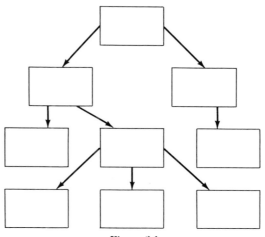

Figure 2.1
Hierarchial structured data base system.

by direct address in the prefix of a record. Moreover, all data fields are referenced by pointers to the data files that contain the segments. IMS/VS, another DBMS classified within the hierarchical approach (because of the concurrent existence of its "logical" data bases or hierarchies that are subsets of IMS/VS), is the most complex system in this category. (For an outline of hierarchical data base system, see Figure 2.1.)

 2. The network approach—in which data is linked into a network structure. Network DBMS such as Total and IDMS provide two levels of entity relations or records: single entry and variable entry (file) records. Each single entry record can have many associative relations or records of multiple variable entry files. Logical relationships among records are set up by indirect pointers that link a single entry record and records in a variable entry file into a two-way circular chain. (For an outline of network data base system, see Figure 2.2.)

 3. The relational approach—in which data are stored in two-dimensional flat files (relations). Relational DBMS such as Infodata Systems' INQUIRE and IQ/Net provide the capability to combine and choose from a set of tuples (group of related fields, i.e., the same data element types) and form different relations. (The tuples are uniquely identified through assigned keys.) The resulting recombined relations are displayed in the user's

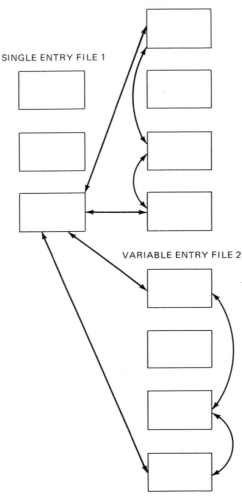
VARIABLE ENTRY FILE 1

SINGLE ENTRY FILE 1

VARIABLE ENTRY FILE 2

Figure 2.2
Network structured data base system.

workspace. (The technique of decomposing complex data structures into relations is called *normalization*.) Though the relational approach requires some redundancy, it does provide great flexibility to the user in manipulating data. (For an outline of relational data base system, see Figure 2.3.)

Insofar as the noncomputer professional user/decision

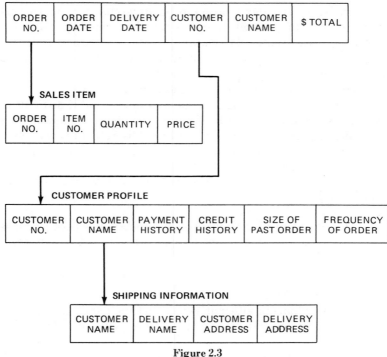

Figure 2.3
Relational structured data base system.

maker is concerned, the main difference between file and data base systems is that the data base can provide timely, accurate information much faster than the file system. And because even a small improvement in the decision-making process can result in reduced costs and more profits, the data base system can assist the user more effectively. (Sample application showing usage of a DBMS is presented on pp. 17–20.)

2.2 TYPES OF DECISIONS AND DECISION MAKERS

Because a major goal in implementing a file management system or a DBMS is to provide efficient access to information for use in the decision-making process, a discussion on decision-making processes and decision makers follows.

9

Admittedly, there is a wide variety of decision-making processes, and even more pronounced diversity among the decision makers. In general, however, at the economic level, decision processes involve determining profit, costs, and risks for alternatives, and finding cost-effective alternatives through a series of limited comparisons. These actions require an assortment of data from various sources and periods of time.

Although most decision makers seem to find it difficult to describe the modus operandi of their decision processes, when they make or present a decision, they usually rely on verbal communication and conceptualization via pictures, different types of charts, and/or slides.

The activities that lead to decision-making may be categorized as follows:

1. Problem finding (exception reports, low profit or loss on a certain product or operation, need for manpower allocation, etc.).

2. Developing of alternatives or plans for solving the problem.

3. Evaluating alternatives or methods and selecting the most cost-effective method to solve the problem.

Because each decision maker has his/her own style, skill, and depth of knowledge, there is a clear difference in the way each decision maker uses and accomplishes the activities above. Nevertheless, the decision makers need extracts of compiled timely data that are relevant to the problem and alternatives.

Although a file management type of Management Information System (MIS) supports—to a certain extent—decision-making, a data base MIS can provide useful information without the decision maker's having to repeat (or have somebody else repeat) the operations that produced the resulting information. The DBMS can also provide—either online or on hard copy—functional graphs that reduce complexities to legible information, so that the decision maker can concentrate on the important issues in making a decision.

In sum, while decision-making is still the responsibility of the decision maker, a well-designed data base system *with* a data dictionary system can give valuable support and shorten the time of collecting and presenting the needed information.

2.3 FILE AND DATA BASE SYSTEMS
EXAMPLES

The remainder of this chapter is devoted to two examples that present clearly the difference between a file and a data base system. In the first example, the file management type of MIS, though satisfying the current corporate management, is weighed down with redundancy of identical data and duplication of programming efforts. Moreover, because everything is batch-processed, management do not receive as timely information for decision-making as if the system could be retrieved and updated in real time. In the second example, on the other hand, the DBMS contains minimal data redundancy, and corporate management are aided in decision-making by directly accessing the system to obtain information about business activities, as well as cost and resource utilization.

FILE MANAGEMENT INFORMATION SYSTEM

BIRD CORPORATION'S MANAGEMENT INFORMATION SYSTEM

Introduction

The Management Information System (MIS) of Bird Corporation, a wholesale supplier of lumber, building materials, and home center products, with a gross revenue of $110 million, is a typical file system. The management, sales staff, home office, and warehouse depend heavily on the company's data processing staff who use an IBM 370/155 OS/VS, 512K, VSAM (Virtual Storage Access Method). The MIS runs on COBOL, except a few utility programs that run on Assembly Language.

System Overview

The Bird Corporation's MIS is designed to process sales orders; control inventory; take care of accounts receivable/accounts payable; keep accurate records of customers' credit, orders, and service; keep a complete history file of each employee, and provide management with reports that show the status of all phases of their operation. The system is comprised of the following subsystems. (An overview diagram in Figure 2.4 of the Bird Corporation's MIS follows.)

   1. Inventory Control Subsystem—The primary function of the Inventory Control Subsystem is to update, change, and main-

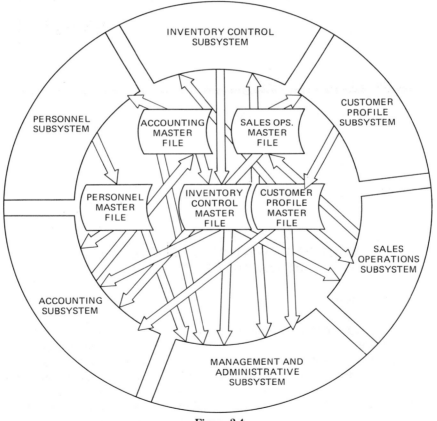

Figure 2.4
Bird corporation's management information system.

14

tain a current and accurate Master Inventory Control File so that its data can be used by the Sales Operations and Accounting subsystems. It generates weekly reports that display recommended orders of quantities of various sales items and carloading patterns based on weekly shipments from the company's warehouse. This subsystem verifies all data elements prior to updating the Master Inventory Control File. Moreover, its effective internal controls and audit trails ensure the integrity of the subsystem's files. The Master File is maintained on disk, while five generations of backup activities are kept on tapes.

   2. Sales Operations Subsystem—The main purpose of this subsystem is to control the company's sales orders; keep a complete history on sales staff and distributors' performance, and provide necessary data for the Inventory Control, Accounting, and Customer Profile subsystems. Certain modules of this subsystem are run daily to maintain an up-to-date Master Sales Operations File (on disk) and generate daily reports.

   3. Customer Profile Subsystem—The major function of the Customer Profile Subsystem is to maintain a current Customer Master File to be used in the Sales Operations, Inventory Control, and Accounting subsystems. The Master File maintained on disk contains up-to-date information such as name, delivery name, address, delivery address, history of payment, credit, size and frequency of orders, last date of order, and type of service about all customers.

   4. Accounting Subsystem—This subsystem uses files maintained in the Inventory Control, Sales Operations, Customer Profile, and Personnel subsystems to process accounts receivable (invoices, credit notes, adjustments, discounts, etc.), accounts payable, payroll, allocation of cash, etc. The Master File (on disk) is updated daily. Most of the programs in the Accounting Subsystem follow a specific sequence in running the jobs; however, some programs are standalones, depending on the input to be processed and the reports to be printed. This subsystem generates daily, weekly, monthly, quarterly, and yearly reports. It also inputs the necessary data to the Management and Administrative Subsystem.

   5. Personnel Subsystem—The primary function of this subsystem is to maintain an up-to-date profile on the employees of Bird Corporation and to provide data for the Accounting and Management and Administrative subsystems. The Master Personnel File (on disk) contains static information such as the employee's name, address, marital status, level of education, ID, and status of life and hospitalization insurance. It also contains current information such as job title, grade, current salary, last review date, last increase amount, and promotion. This subsystem generates a variety of reports *on request.*

6. Management and Administrative Subsystem—The purpose of this subsystem is to provide management with reliable and timely statistical sales-performance and forecasting reports. These reports support planning and decision-making, and provide an overview of the company's operations. In other words, this subsystem is a management tool for monitoring the enterprise's operations in toto.

DATA BASE
MANAGEMENT
INFORMATION SYSTEM

BESCL'S DATA BASE MANAGEMENT
INFORMATION SYSTEM

Introduction

BESCL (Banco Esperito Santo e Comercial de Lisboa) is one of the largest banks in Portugal. It has 35 branches in greater Lisbon and another 120 throughout the country. BESCL was the first Portuguese bank to implement an online multiprocessing data base network Management Information System. The data base, under the control of DMS 1100 (Data Management System 1100)—a CODASYL System, i.e., an information management system based upon the specifications of the CODASYL Data Base Task Group—is implemented on a

Univac 1100/12, 1.5MB, OS1100 multiprocessor. The programming language used is PL/I.

Prior to this system, BESCL used a conventional file system. Moreover, all bank transactions at the branches were done manually. Specifically, a card was maintained for each customer at the appropriate branch. Every credit and debit transaction was recorded on the customer's card, each line containing the current total. The actual recording was done by inserting the card into an accounting machine (each branch had two or three accounting machines) and keying in the data. The accounting machine, in addition to recording transactions on the cards, generated paper tapes containing one record per activity. At the end of each working day the tellers checked their totals on the accounting machines; the branch managers balanced the data on the paper tapes against the source documents and sent the paper tapes by in-house mail to the bank's Computer Center on Rua Castilho in Lisbon. At the Center, the data on paper tapes were transferred to magnetic tapes and then to disks, and processed in batch mode on a Univac 90/70 VS/9 VDU System (512K). On this file management system all account files were held centrally and updated on disks. Summary reports and monthly statements were generated and mailed semiautomatically to the customers, and daily, weekly, monthly, quarterly, and yearly reports were generated for the management of the bank in order to keep them informed on the status of the bank's operations.

System Overview

Central to the Univac 1100/12 multiprocessor system is a centralized data base, a nationwide teleprocessing distributed network with dual front end message switching processors (one is *live;* one is the *backup*), and internal banking CRT terminals. (A detailed configuration of the system appears in Figure 2.5.)

All the 155 branches of BESCL have one Programmable Control Unit (PCU) minicomputer, three to ten administrative and tele-terminals, and a printer-validation logging device that produces two copies of all transactions. One copy stays inside this sealed device, and the second, visible copy is for checking against possible local errors. The PCU software handles the screen formats, the field checking, and check digits, and maintains locally the totals of the tellers and of the branch.

The bank tellers, using a command language, are putting

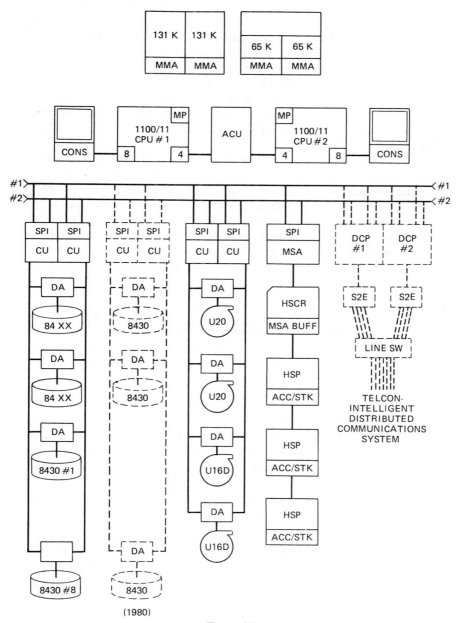

(1980)

Figure 2.5
BESCL's Univac 1100/12 multiprocessing system configuration.
(Courtesy Banco Espirito Santo e Comercial)

through all transactions in real time; that is, the PCU checks each transaction and if the input data is valid, it sends a compressed message of the data to the host computer at BESCL's DP Center in Lisbon. The host computer processes the transaction in real time, updates the data base under the control of DMS 1100, and sends an acknowledgment to the teller's terminal. The terminal remains locked until the host computer replies. (The average response time is 3–4 seconds.)

Management, in addition to receiving both summary and detailed reports in a timely fashion about every phase of the banking operation, has the use of OPTIMA 1100. This is a flexible project management system that provides data about networks of activities, time analysis, cost and resource utilization, and performing resource allocation in extensive reports. OPTIMA 1100—a feature of the data base—is utilized via a command language.

The security of BESCL Data Base Management Information System consists of the following:

1. There is a mechanical lock on the PCU. The branch manager is the only person who has the key.

2. The branch manager maintains a list of valid passwords (that he changes periodically) for that particular branch.

3. The PCU checks the password as each bank teller logs in.

4. The passwords and the teller's ID are sent to the host computer with every transaction.

5. The branch amount and the tellers' totals are checked out, as well as the branch totals and the PCU totals. In addition, the host computer totals are checked against the branch totals.

6. Any discrepancy is checked against the transaction log that contains the teller's ID and the transaction sequence number.

7. Each transaction is recorded twice: once in the sealed validation printer at the branch and a second time in the transaction log file in the host computer. Thus, there are two constant audit trails.

8. The amount of money a teller can handle depends on his/her security level, which is implicit in the password structure.

3

WHAT IS
A DATA DICTIONARY
SYSTEM?

For the enterprise to be effective, it must manage all its resources, including data. By gaining control over its data resource, the organization goes a long way to effect a productive and cost-beneficial management information system. And the best tool to accomplish this is a data dictionary system, preferably with on-line update and reporting features. (In a batch environment one can never be sure that the reports are up to date). By collecting, verifying, storing, and—under stringent security regulations—disseminating information about the enterprise's data, a DDS enables management to control and optimize a valuable corporate resource: data.

Since a data dictionary means different things to people

on different position levels within the enterprise's hierarchy, it is described in terms of its usefulness to the following:

1. Management
2. Auditors
3. Data administrators
4. System analysts/designers
5. Programmers
6. Operations staff

3.1 DATA DICTIONARY CAPABILITIES

Before describing the levels of use of a data dictionary system, it is essential to emphasize that the DDS does *not* contain the actual data of the enterprise, nor does it describe the content (i.e., the applications of a conventional file system or a data base). It records and disseminates (through reports and online query) *information* about data: specifically, information about the origins of data, data attributes, usage, location, format, relationships, and dispositions. Thus, the DDS is a centralized repository, a library, if you will, of coherent information about all aspects of different types and structures of data residing in data bases and/or file systems and/or manual systems. It stores information about data elements and data items used within records, files, tuples (as in relational DBMS), Codasyl sets, and IMS segments.

It is interesting to note that the current concept of a data dictionary system is a composite of the following:

Data catalog: a structured listing of data elements with or without a description of the listed elements.

Data dictionary: an organized compilation of data elements, data items, attributes, structure, and characteristics.

Data directory: an orderly listing of data element names, identifiers, locations, and physical characteristics of these data.

Data dictionary/directory: A collection of data elements, informational entities, structure, characteristics, and locations of data. Thus, it combines the features of a data dictionary and data directory.

There are two types of data dictionary systems: (1) a stand-alone, self-contained DDS that has its own maintenance and reporting programs and (2) a DDS that is implemented as an application of and consequently dependent on a data base or a DBMS to function.

A stand-alone DDS can support one or more DBMS through interfaces. Such a DDS enables the data administrator to exercise tight control over the DBMS. A dependent DDS is more often than not a commercially available package, designed for a general-purpose DBMS. This is not to say that a DBMS-dependent DDS is more difficult to develop in house than a stand-alone system. It is not. Both types of data dictionaries, however, take careful planning, meticulous designing and testing, and proper implementation, just as a DBMS.

3.2 PROS AND CONS OF STAND-ALONE AND DEPENDENT DDSs

Both types of DDSs have their pros and cons. For example, the stand-alone DDS can have the capability to edit and verify all data entities before storing them, thus ensuring consistency in data definitions. Conversely, the dependent DDS does not have the capability to clean up inconsistent data definitions that exist in the already implemented DBMS. Also, whereas the stand-alone DDS—whether developed in house or bought as a package—has great flexibility and portability, the dependent DDS is restricted to a particular DBMS.

On the other hand, a DDS that is part of a DBMS can contribute to the system's optimization by generating control blocks and supplying a comprehensive inventory of DBMS and non-DBMS files, nonstandard procedures, and COBOL Copylibs. Then again, the stand-alone DDS can provide some of the same functions to one or more DBMS through interfaces. Thus, some conclusions may be drawn as to circumstances where one type is preferable over the other. The dependent DDS can be useful in a situation where all operational data is stored under a single DBMS. But in multiple DBMSs, or other situations, the standalone DDS may be the only tool that can provide centralized control of all data.

The DDS is maintained by the following:

- Transactions that support and report on the status of DDS.

- Software that collects and edits input from directories and compilers, and generates input required by the operational environment.

- Applications that perform consistency control and, in the more sophisticated data dictionaries, generate change impact analysis.

To supply the enterprise a complete scenario of its data processing functions, as well as an in-depth profile of its resource data, the DDS can provide the following:

- Description of unique identifications and physical characteristics of each data element and data item within the organization.

- Information as to the source, location, usage, and destination of each entity, as well as to the creation of a new entity whenever that occurs.

- Retrieval and cross-referencing capabilities. Through its command language, the DDS can retrieve information online or in batch mode through keywording, indexing, or other methods.

- Accurate picture of the relationships of data to other data, of data to data structures (e.g., data bases and files), of data to processes and processing structures (e.g., systems and programs), of data to processing (e.g., transactions), and of data to reports.

- Validation and redundancy checking capabilites.

- Support functions in conversion to new data processing environments such as from conventional file system to single DBMS, from file system or single DBMS to distributed data processing, and from single DBMS to multi-DBMSs.

- Naming standardization, an essential factor for handling and controlling the data resource.

- Capability to read (though not directly) the DBMS directory, thus providing users the most current information about data in the DBMS.

- COBOL Copylib generation.

- Capability to ensure that when production JCL is changed, there is a corresponding change in the file system or data base.

- Estimates as to the possible cost and time scale of any proposed changes to the file system or data base.

- Facilities to interact with one or more DBMS.

- Consistent and timely documentation.

- Reporting facilities. These reports may include the following:

  - Data usage reports.

  - Change-impact reports, i.e., documents that report on proposed as well as actual changes, and how they affect files, modules, segments, programs, and records.

  - Cross-reference reports.

  - Error reports.

  - Ad hoc reports.

  - Audit-trail reports.

  - Security reports, i.e., reports on security measures as to who can access sensitive data and information, thus supporting the internal control function.

In a DBMS environment, in addition to the capabilities listed above, the DDS can become the source of generating data management control language, as well as schema* and sub-schema**. Thus, for example, if the DBMS operates in only one

*Schema = a defining and describing of the total data base to the user.
**Subschema = a defining and describing of particular subsets of interest to the user.

programming language, the DDS may be employed as the input at the source (subschema) level or at the subroutine library level for generation of alternative facilities.

3.3 DATA DICTIONARY USERS

Because one of the "selling points" of the DDS is its ability to provide different features to different users, the following sections delineate the various user categories and the distinct characteristics offered to them by the data dictionary.

3.3.1 Management

A successful enterprise is the mirror of an effective management. And a vigorous management is cognizant of the value of corporate resources, and optimizes and safeguards them accordingly. Yet, until quite recently only a small percentage of enterprises exercised as tight a control over their data resource as over their other resources such as cash, stocks, equipment, personnel, and real estate. Perhaps too many organizations gave credence to the modern fairy tale that having a DBMS is a panacea to all their security troubles.

In any case, now the DDS, an easily accessible and valuable management tool, can enforce security safeguards (measures) against any accidental or intentional unauthorized use of confidential data.

In addition to the previously discussed primary functions, the DDS, under the direction of a data administrator, can provide management the following:

• Information about existing corporate data across divisions, departments, and applications.

• Information as to how and where, i.e., in what processes these data are being used.

• A means for controlling existing and new data, and controlling new uses and/or modifications of existing data or processes that are using these data.

• An effective tool for standardization of data definitions.

Because standards are a basic part of the DDS, enforcement of data definition standards is facilitated for management. Standards, if enforced, will eliminate data redundancy, as well as errors caused by contradictory data definitions. This is critical, especially after a conversion or merger, when it is difficult to control data definitions and formats. Finally, with the provided security measures, a DDS ensures that the valuable corporate data resource is safeguarded.

3.3.2 Auditors

Both inside and outside government auditors are concerned with the control and accuracy of information about the flow of data, finances, and operations throughout the enterprise. The company auditor in addition needs to audit and evaluate new/revised systems for effectiveness, reliability, and timeliness. The online data dictionary, being a centralized warehouse for all possible information about the enterprise, provides the auditors a quick and effective mechanism to trace and audit all activities with which they are concerned.

3.3.3 Data Administrator

Because the data administrator's primary responsibilities are to control data definition and use in all applications, and ensure that new applications use existing data, a data dictionary system is an excellent device for handling these functions.

When a DDS is operating in a non-DBMS environment, it is the data administrator (DA) who ensures that analysts/designers, programmers, and other users are provided a communications framework for whatever data and processing structures they need. It is also the DA who polices the access to sensitive data in the data dictionary.

In a DBMS environment, the data base administrator (who may also be the dictionary DA) has the responsibility for implementing and maintaining both the DBMS and the DDS. Controlling the consistency of entries—a DDS function—is imperative in either environment. In a distributed data processing environment, whether the administration of the distributed data base is "central control," "local control," or "local operations control-central procedural control," a data dictionary can be very useful. When a data base is reorganized or restructured for more efficiency, or because of changes in the user environment or changes in the facility's hardware or software or any other reasons, a DDS is invaluable. Not only can it serve as an inventory of the old and new data, but it can create tables that will match old data elements and data items and relationships with new data elements and data items and describe these relationships.

A DDS provides the data administrator with the following:

- An effective means for recording in detail and uniformly information about both DBMS and non-DBMS systems as well as manual systems.

- A valuable tool for monitoring changes. Because the data dictionary can record details of current changes as well as proposed changes, it can alert the DA to any inconsistencies and show the impact of current and proposed changes on files, programs, and reports.

- A device for estimating major cost factors in implementing planned modifications. Based on such information, the DA can recommend, if necessary, a more cost-effective implementation procedure.

- A facility that optimizes the use of corporate data.

- A media through which he/she can acquaint the non-data processing staff with appropriate corporate data. This will utilize all the functions performed in the enterprise as well as facilitate the DA to fulfill his role as a liaison between non-DP and DP staff.

  - Description of the data base.

  - Subschema generation.

  - Data description for application programs.

  - Extensive and timely online documentation of all data structures.

Because security and privacy are crucial in both DBMS

and non-DBMS environments, it is the function of the DA to place constraints on the DDS. In other words, since the DDS is used as an access control, correspondingly, the DDS must be subject to control measures also. Thus it is the data administrator's responsibility to enforce the rule that all dictionary updates, additions, or deletions are performed by standardized transactions under the same control. In addition, it is the function and responsibility of the DA to restrict the number of non-DP users who may have access to sensitive data within the DDS. And it is the data administrator who limits the number of analysts and programmers allowed to update/modify the contents of the DDS.

3.3.4 Systems Analyst/Designer

Because the systems analyst/designer has to know the data resource of the enterprise, the data needed for processing, and the information of how that processing affects the data entities and the organization, the DDS can become a powerful software tool for system development by providing the information above in an accurate and expeditious manner.

Specifically, a DDS can be used in systems analysis, design, and implementation stages for the following:

- Verification of the basic structure of the enterprise's data, as well as the manner in which events and functions use these data.

- Inquiry and analysis as to what metadata (data about data) and functions need to be gathered for the system development.

- Analysis of the data elements and data items within *and* without the existing traditional file systems and/or DBMS to obtain an accurate picture of the system structure, analysis of the entities' attributes, relationships, estimates of usage patterns, frequencies, and security measures.

- Identification and analysis of contradictory and erroneous data usages.

- Identification and removal of redundant data from the file system and/or data base.

- Implementation of standardized procedures to ensure consistent method in updating the new or modified file system or data base.

- Documentation of the system during the development cycle. Moreover, because the DDS documentation is reliable and automated, the new or modified system documentation will be much easier to update and keep current than it might be with most text-editing or manual documentation systems.

- Definitions of traditional files and conversion transactions in case there is a need for generating file management utilities.

- Interface function between the file system or the DBMS and the users, in user-oriented formats.

- Recording conclusions or decisions about certain aspects of the system that is being analyzed and designed, as well as a reference to other systems' data.

- Description of manual files, conventional computer files, DBMS segments, and the applications/processes that sustain the systems.

- Descriptions of processing areas such as Codasyl schemas and subschemas—if working with a DBMS.

- Automatic copy definitions and generations of entries from information in COBOL and PL/I programs, as well as schema and subschemas—if the DDS is an application of a DBMS.

- Descriptions of all versions of programs and files for quick access to backup files and programs and for controlling file generation.

- Description of both the initial and dynamic physical characteristics of the files, as well as their "operating system address."

To assist the systems analyst further, a dictionary can also provide information about the following:

- Functions and responsibilities of particular of users.
- Privacy constraint and security measures.

- Progress as to the development of the new system or the modification of the current system.

- Status of the project documentation.

- Latest recorded version of the conceptual* and the implementation** views. (For a detailed discussion of these views, see Chapter 5.)

The conceptual view or level is quite important to the systems analyst who is developing a system, since his system (especially if it is a DBMS) to be useful must be a model of the using organization. Equally important to the systems analyst is obtaining definitive information about the major functions and resource entities of the enterprise without the information being colored by a particular division's/department's implementation view of these entities and functions. In fact, unambiguous statements of the enterprise's data needs, without presuming storage structures or access methods, are essential for the design of an effective system. Such statements are also critical in the conversion of manual files to traditional computer files, traditional files to a single DBMS, modification of existing single DBMS, and conversion of single DBMS to multi-DBMSs.

3.3.5 Programmer

At most installations, program updating, modifications, and changes to the data structures is a continuous process. Consequently, the maintenance programmer must have easy access to all versions of programs and data structures.

A DDS can provide the programmer with the following:

- Description of common source code stored in the dictionary.

- Information about interdependencies.

- Description of the usage of a particular program in various systems.

*Conceptual view = a description of the framework within which the enterprise exists and operates and within which the analyst's system will have to function.
**Implementation view = a description of the stage within which the system is made operational.

- Description of the usage of data entities in various programs.

- Description of files and the programs accessing them.

- Description of relationships between data entities and programs.

- Generation of data descriptions for COBOL and PL/I.

- Automatic description of the file/task relationship and program/data relationships.

- The updated version of cross-references of data entities used by particular programs and accessed by other programs.

- Definitive information about the form and usage of data in the implementation stage, thus giving the programmer a means of quality control for the programs in production. In other words, the programmer does not have to check whether the programs use the correct and allowed data; the DDS does it automatically for him or her.

- Generation of reporting utilities.

- Quality control insofar as checking and confirming the validation procedures of each item in the system per the established validation rules stored in the DDS.

- Essential facilities for data capture, consistency checking, access, and reporting.

- Information on all versions of programs and data structures, i.e., the design, test, and live versions of programs and data structures of all existing systems.

3.3.6 Operations Staff

While the conceptual level is a definition of the framework within which the enterprise exists and the implementation scenario is the description of the data entities and their functions as they relate to files and programs, the operational stage provides the basic information about physical files and data used in the operating system. Consequently, the operations staff needs source information about the systems to be implemented, physical files of these systems, jobs to be run, and relationships between programs and data structures. Simply put, the systems analyst may design a highly effective and cost-beneficial system, but if the operational scene is not consistent with itself and the implementation scenario, the system will fail and the many man-months of effort will be wasted.

A DDS can provide certain information for the operations staff, which then can help them in the following:

- Scheduling jobs. This being a critical function of operations, it is important that all I/O processing is accurate and consistent, and that job processing is efficient. The information supplied by DDS allows this function to be accurate and involve minimal manual work.

- Controlling file generations.

- Validating input. By checking the characteristics and content of each physical file as well as each physical data structure accessed by the processing programs, the DDS verifies the input for syntax, accuracy, and consistency with the implementation concept.

- Gathering performance statistics.

- Automatic generation of information about physical files and data structures.

- Automatic generation of production JCL (Job Control Language).

- Ensuring that with a change in production JCL there is a corresponding change performed in the file system or data base.

- Recording the allocation of physical resources.

DDS can supply operations staff with reports that may include the following:

- Listings of the latest version of operational files.

- Listings of the latest version of programs and jobs they are running.

- Listings of transactions and processing units.

- Cross-references between operational files and the programs accessing them.

DDS can help in reducing if not eliminating manual work for the operations staff by storing and maintaining descriptions of all versions of files and programs. These capabilities of the data dictionary facilitates operations staff in retrieving backup files and programs in case of emergency. In most facilities, crises can and will happen quite often, if not with frustrating regularity. Use of a DDS in an operational environment minimizes the impact of such events.

4

BENEFITS
OF THE DATA
DICTIONARY

Because an online data dictionary can be truly a controlled information system, its most obvious benefit is of providing its users valid, uniform, and continually updated information on all aspects of the enterprise's operations. Through its capability of recording and maintaining descriptive information about data in a centralized library, it facilitates data sharing. It provides information on how specific programs utilize particular data elements and their attributes, and which files contain these data. It informs the user as to the source (department, form, etc.) of the data, as well as the frequency and sequence of use of these data. And because any update/change to a program/module or file/segment must be signed off by the data administrator, unauthorized updates/changes cannot enter the system.

Further, the DDS provides a structure and a set of rules for manipulating and documenting the enterprise's data. This in turn results in better documentation, which then facilitates future modification and conversion requirements of the application systems.

Management of organizations that develop a DDS alongside a conventional non-DBMS system can use the data dictionary as a tool to help to overcome possible organizational and psychological problems with the planned "going Data Base" concept. A second less obvious (nevertheless important) benefit of DDS is its role as an effective mechanism in aiding to dispel the still-existing myth that data is the property of the data processing organization. The fact is that data is an enterprise resource, and a valuable one at that.

In short, the data dictionary's major benefits derive from its flexibility to changes and its centralized location. These capabilities allow the DDS to provide stringently controlled information on how and where particular data originated and to permit tracking of when, where, how frequently, and in what sequence these data and their attributes are being used. Use of the DDS thereby reduces costs both for maintenance of the existing data and for making system modifications involving that data.

4.1 CONSTRAINING FACTORS

To effect the many benefits of DDS—not the least of which is providing better data for decision-making—management must be cognizant and act upon several constraining factors before allowing the development of a DDS.

These constraints are:

4.1.1 Revolutionary Philosophy

The enterprise, and more specifically all levels of management, must understand that unless they recognize that DDS represents a revolutionary philosophy, little or no benefits will be derived from this system. They must be aware that DDS—if well designed, carefully implemented, and properly used—is a central controlling mechanism for all aspects of the enterprise's operating systems and can impact every department in the organization. The data dictionary is not just an automated version of the manual data element catalog that lists data elements alphabetically and cross-references them with data element numbers. The DDS is an online data base for data about data (metadata if you will) and as such is a powerful management tool.

Conversely, DDS of inferior design, careless implementation, and haphazard usage will compound instead of alleviate problems such as data redundancy; errors in values or no assigned values at all; inaccurate data definitions; inconsistency in COBOL pictures, mnemonics and synonyms; and ignoring of standards. Data that are not verified when input to the DDS and then copied and recopied with all the errors in them, can become a formidable problem, to say the least.

4.1.2 Commitment

Management must be committed to the DDS and all its constraints. In other words, if the users within the enterprise have been used to "doing their own thing" insofar as changing input documents (forms), recompiling programs, or updating/modifying files without submitting their changes for review and approval to a central controlling person—the department manager or the data administrator (DA)—management must stop such practices. Simply put, if management wants to utilize fully the capabilities of the dictionary, like reducing the volume of data to be managed by eliminating unplanned data redundancies and thus increasing the productivity of both human and machine resources, for example, they have to be committed to the system and resist any *exceptions* to the disciplining imposed on the organization by DDS. That is not to say that without a DDS management cannot establish standards. With a DDS, however, it is much easier to enforce such controls.

4.1.3 Restricting the Programmers' Work Area

To ensure that only valid, authorized updates/changes are input to the system, application and maintenance programmers are to be restricted to work with the Test Library. The tested updates/changes to programs/modules and files/segments contained in the Test Library are subsequently to be given to the department manager or the DA for review, approval, and sign off. And

only after the DDS accesses for the latest metadata are these up-
dates/changes to be input to the Production Libraries. Limiting
applications programmers' work area to the Test Library does
not mean that they are not allowed to access data in the system.
They can and should access files and programs. However, by
using the "sign off" approach, the possibility of unauthorized up-
dates/changes are reduced to minimum; thus higher security and
data integrity are achieved.

4.1.4 Creating the Data Administrator Function

Because the function of the DA (to service and control the enterprise data pool by ensuring that the rules and regulations of DDS
are maintained and enforced) is essential, management must
create this office. And not after a dictionary is implemented but
early in its planning stage. Actually, without a DA it is doubtful
whether a dictionary can be maintained and be of any use to the
enterprise.

4.2 BENEFITS OF THE DATA DICTIONARY

Given that management decides to accept the constraints,
numerous benefits may be realized through development of a
data dictionary system. These benefits include the following:

4.2.1 Minimizing Data Redundancy

Whenever a new system or application is being designed and
developed—unless there is a centralized online DDS—the
systems designers may create a number of already existing data
elements. This can happen when the systems designers do not
know that the same data have been defined before, that these
data already exist in another system or application's records.
Moreover, the designer may assign these data slightly different
COBOL names and values than the existing data have. When the
organization has a DDS, such redundancy is greatly minimized,
which in turn reduces data base space requirement, thus conserv-
ing hardware resources. Not only can the designer query the DDS
as to whether such data have been created before and ask for an
in-depth profile on each, but the DDS can block any attempt to

insert a data element or data item that is already in the systems and about which information is stored in the dictionary.

In cases where for convenience or for design purposes the decision is to allow data redundancy, such occurrences are documented and referenced in the DDS. For example, in a certain insurance company's system the data element SECURITY CODE is assigned three different numbers, three different definitions, and three different range of values. According to the designer, this code's values and definitions depend on the claim type. Still, each of them is SECURITY CODE, and so the DDS deliberately permits this data redundancy.

4.2.2 Relationships

Most mature data processing facilities have one or more data bases and a few conventional files, or a file management system. It is not unusual to have similar types of data elements in the data base and in various applications. In such cases, and in cases where the same data type is known by other names, the DDS can be used to inform the users of the relationships that exist among these data and of the disposition of their usage. In other words, the DDS provides information as to which modules/programs and systems use the same data type and how they relate.

4.2.3 Data Integrity

Because the DDS contains comprehensive and constantly updated information about the enterprise's data and its usage, and because of the strict standards that DDS must be operated by in order to be useful, it can provide better data integrity than a file management system or any variety of data bases.

4.2.4 Data Tracking

The tracking of how programs/modules use particular data as well as which files/segments contain certain data is extremely important to the systems analyst in performing system changes. Through the DDS, he/she is able to ascertain what impact the proposed changes will have on other components of the system and upon functional areas within the enterprise. By having an accurate, up-to-date assessment of the location and usage of data that will be involved in the system change, the analyst can accomplish the task more efficiently.

4.2.5 System Maintenance

Because easy access to information about system changes as well as reliable documentation and consistency and adherence to standards are essential for system maintenance and because the data dictionary provides both such access and product, it is invaluable to programmers. To put it another way, because DDS provides automatic standards for enforcement, the maintenance programmers are assured of data uniformity, and consequently they quite justly feel that they can rely upon the information provided by DDS as to data usability. Thus here too, by simplifying and automating repetitive and error-prone tasks, DDS cuts lead time and cost. Also, DDS makes maintenance programmers' work less of a chore. This is a notable point, considering that it is rather difficult to hold onto good maintenance programmers.

4.2.6 Control of Data

Perhaps one of the most important benefits of DDS is that because it gives accurate and timely information, management can control more efficiently not only the automated and manual data of the enterprise but all its resources and operations. Consequently, management is provided with precise and accurate data for quick, profitable decision-making.

CASE IN POINT:

Thomas E. Murray, Manager, Information Services Development, Del Monte Corporation, San Francisco, has this to say about Del Monte's approach for the control of corporate data and the establishing of a DDS within their planned and successfully carried out 1974–80 time frame.

> While we have implemented several major applications with our CINCOM's TOTAL DBMS, we have given greater emphasis in the short term to getting control of our overall corporate data resource. After having tried in 1968 a manually-fed Data Element Catalog, which proved costly to maintain and was never up to date (and so was shelved), we embarked in 1974 on establishing an

automated data dictionary to interrelate procedures, programs, reports, files, data elements, etc., directly from our production job control procedures, COBOL COPY Library data definitions, MARK IV glossaries, and TOTAL data definitions. This encompasses all of our systems and data—not just the newly-evolving DBMS-based applications. Thus, the effort covered almost everything processed on our central IBM 370/158: close to 2,000 programs, 1,700 reports and 7,500 reels of data on tape, as well as those data sets resident on about a dozen 3330/3350 disk spindles. Interestingly enough, our *unique* data elements in the final count were less than 700.

Many organizations have gotten into Data Base without fully recognizing the need for a DDS; others have used a DDS only in connection with a specific DBMS-based data. Often, the rationale was that it would take too much time and money to create a more global DDS. Many of these same organizations have since found the need to install the broader DDS. Actually, if an organization can't afford this, maybe the company can't really afford a Data Base (or maybe the company just doesn't know what Data Base itself will cost).

An astute MIS director I know once described a Management Information System as a *replication* of the real business enterprise, which had become too extensive and complex to manage in the old way—by first-hand inspection. In a very real sense, our present-day computer-based information systems—with or without DBMS—have become so complex and interwoven in themselves that we can no longer manage them without first representing them in an accurate model of the data resource, such as by use of an automated data dictionary.

4.2.7 Reference

As a reference and cross-reference tool, DDS is invaluable to both middle DP management and programmers. Because of its cross-reference and inquiry capabilities, DDS is a great help to project leaders in evaluating the impact of a proposed change prior to its implementation. And because DDS contains detailed definitions of data elements and their complete attributes, specifically: their size, type, characteristics (alpha, numeric, or alphanumeric), their usage (internally stored in binary or packed decimal, etc.), logical and physical locations, valid ranges of values for each element, how the bits are stored, and the interrelationships between the same type of data in various systems or applications, it aids the programmers. Also, DDS contains information about the reports in which the referenced data appear. In addition, if DDS contains definitions of source codes, object codes, and procedure codes, it can be referenced and used by the programmer in generating object codes as well as source codes to be used for sysgens (systems generations) in the operating system.

4.2.8 Costs and Reduction of Lead Time

By having centrally maintained inventory of information about the enterprise's data and its operations, a reduction in lead time as well as costs is effected. Specifically, by using the online access for description of data definitions and the DDS capability to generate control blocks and program input/output areas automatically and accurately, new system/application development time is reduced. Also, changes/modifications can be accomplished more quickly and correctly by using the information in the DDS as to the usage and relationships of data entities and programs, as well as files and the programs accessing them.

4.2.9 Standards and Documentation

Because adherence to standards is a requisite for a functional dictionary, developing and enforcing standards throughout the organization is easier with a DDS. Moreover, the data dictionary can be made to provide quality documentation—in both content and form. If documentation is left to individuals in various data processing department sections, the probability of producing the same high-quality documentation consistently is quite small.

4.2.10 Security

DDS can offer an added benefit in the security area for controlling the access to information about corporate resource and dictionary functions by dynamically allocating passwords to users. The passwords are time-limited and purged from the dictionary periodically. In addition, DDS can also have a log file that automatically records every inquiry that is being made into sensitive files and data. A report on such monitoring can be important to security, to auditors, and to statistical projects.

4.2.11 Management of Data

If efficient data management means utilizing data and information about data so that it can effect smooth internal operations *and* profit for the enterprise in the competitive marketplace, then this may be best accomplished by the DA. In fact, it is one of his/her responsibilities to manage and coordinate the different data requirements of both the "owners" and the "users" of data.

Owners of data are the divisions/departments/shops/warehouses within the organization where the particular data generated. Owners' data may be unique to the activities of a division/department/shop or warehouse, or it may be shared between departments, as in the case of employee records shared by the Personnel and Payroll Departments. The *users of data* are the systems analysts and programmers who manipulate and process these data to satisfy the owners' data processing requirements and to aid management in decision-making.

Through the use of a centralized data dictionary system, the DA can provide and enforce standards complying with the requests of both *owners* and *users of data.* A well-designed DDS that is controlled and maintained by a competent DA can provide a level of management of the corporate data resource that would be quite difficult to achieve by other methods.

CONTENTS
AND FUNCTIONS
OF A DATA DICTIONARY
SYSTEM

Since a dictionary can range from the simplest of applications that are stored in a conventional file or a set of files to a comprehensive DDS that is the focal point of a DBMS and stored in a data base, its content and functions vary greatly. The scope, size, and complexity of a DDS depends on the type and size of the enterprise in which the DDS is to be established, the predefined functions of the DDS, and the type of data processing facility that serves the enterprise. The contents and functions of various types of DDS are described in this chapter; the development and installation phases as well as the operations methods are detailed in subsequent chapters.

A DDS that is designed to respond to the user needs, to the particular environment, and to the security and privacy requirements of that environment will identify, define, and describe all the data of the enterprise. It will also provide a structure and a set of rules/procedures for manipulating the data, so that the user needs to deal with only "his view" of a file or data element, or other structure. Moreover, through the DDS he can change "his view" (the part of the file or COBOL mnemonic or synonym that he needs) *without* changing other files or the data base itself. However, full utilization of this information processing tool can be achieved only if all the factors mentioned above are studied, defined, evaluated, and structured accordingly.

5.1 TWO VIEWS OF THE ENTERPRISE

Before discussing the contents of various levels of data dictionaries, it is essential to make a distinction between the data requirements of the enterprise's functions and the data requirements of the data processing facilities that support those functions. Therefore, to establish a truly comprehensive dictionary, it is quite important to define and input to DDS the two separate yet related views of the organization. They are (1) the conceptual view and (2) the implementation view.

   1. The conceptual view—encompasses the functions of the enterprise such as marketing, acquiring new contracts or customers and hiring staff. All these functions are independent of any data processing applications. Thus, the conceptual view describes the type of enterprise, the functions it performs, and various data and events that are of interest to the organization. Putting it another way, the conceptual view is a model of the company and its operation.

   The conceptual view contains the following:

- *Enterprise attributes.* Records of data about attributes considered valuable by the organization. These may be property, resources, or people.
- *Enterprise functions.* Data about "lifeline" functions of the organization.
- *Enterprise events.* Data about important events that may influence the direction or policy of the organization.

Enterprise relationships. Definitions of how the organization attributes, functions, and events relate to each other. Statements as to who is authorized to have access to confidential data belong here also.

Without a definition of the relationship between the enterprises's two views, however, much of the value of the defined conceptual view is lost. Consequently, it is particularly important to map the relationship between the enterprise's functions and the modules, programs, systems, etc., of the implementation view.

2. The implementation view—includes descriptions of data base systems, conventional file management systems, and even manual files, as well as information about all processes or applications that support the requirements of the conceptual view. Because the implementation view in fact describes the supporting services it provides for the conceptual view, it cannot have a greater scope than the latter view.

The implementation view contains the following information:

1. How often particular applications are used, and the accessing paths they follow—the DDS can use this data for simple predictions of the machine resources required by indicating the applications' use of the system. This information then may be analyzed by the DA for more detailed predictions of machine resources required.

2. Form and usage of data—having this information enables the DDS to provide quality control by ensuring that programs are using the proper and allowed data and forms.

3. Validation rules—having the validation rules for data enables the DDS to perform validation of the data and of reporting exceptions to the data administrator. Since one of the responsibilities of the DA—as described in a previous chapter—is to enforce quality control by checking the adequacy and correctness of the system's validation procedures, the DDS can be an invaluable aid to the DA.

Again, the scope, size, and complexity of a DDS depends on factors unique to the particular environment. Nevertheless, although some types of data dictionaries overlap, they fall into one of these categories:

5.2 CATEGORIES OF DATA DICTIONARIES

5.2.1 Basic Data Dictionary System

As noted previously, at this level the DDS is nothing more than an automated manual data dictionary. It stands alone, and its function is to list and maintain production data elements and their barest attributes. Even the simplest DDS, however, should provide, in addition to the one-page-per-data-element printout (see Figure 5.1), an alphabetical listing of data elements that cross-references a numerical listing of data elements as well as a COBOL mnemonic index that cross-references the data element numbers. The basic type of DDS contains the following:

Data element names: the unique names given to predefined data fields in records, data sets or files, programs, reports, and forms, for example, ZIP CODE.

Data element numbers: the numbers assigned to specific data elements.

Data Element Name:	CLIENT ID NUMBER
Data Element Number:	10031
COBOL Mnemonic:	ID NO.
COBOL Picture:	X(13)
Definition:	A number to uniquely identify a client.
VALUE	**DESCRIPTION**
A	Commercial
B	Private
C	Unknown

Figure 5.1
Example of a BASIC DICTIONARY SYSTEM output.

COBOL mnemonics: the assigned COBOL names for particular data elements. They are usually identical with the data element names, but they also can be acronyms of these names. For example, often the COBOL mnemonic of the data element name DATE OF BIRTH is DOB.

COBOL pictures: the fields assigned to particular data. For example, 9(5) (numeric) can be assigned for data element ZIP CODE that currently consists of five numbers, 07632, for example; whereas X(7) (alpha) can be assigned for data element FIRST NAME. COBOL pictures may be numeric, alpha, or alphanumeric.

Definition of data elements: the concise and accurate definition of data elements. For example, the definition for data element SOCIAL SECURITY NUMBER may be "The number used by Social Security Administration (SSA) throughout a wage earner's lifetime to identify earnings under the Social Security Program."

Value and description of data elements: the valid range of values as well as description of the values for a specific data element. For example, for the data element DATES OF SERVICE the values and their descriptions may be as follows:

Value	Description
' '	Date of Service Valid
'X'	Date of Service Invalid

5.2.2 Average Data Dictionary System

At this level the DDS becomes more useful, because in addition to the basic components of data element name and number, COBOL mnemonic and picture, and data element definition, and valid codes and their meaning, it contains many more entities. It also has many more capabilities and is able to provide much more service to both computer and noncomputer type of users. The average DDS may be a stand-alone system or it may be a dependent system, i.e., part of a data base. Input to the average DDS may be the following:

- Directly by authorized dictionary users who may use an input language.

- Captured from existing machine readable sources, e.g., program data definitions in high-level languages such as COBOL or PL/1.

- From program procedure statements.

The average DDS is comprised of the following:

Data element names: as defined for basic DDS.

Data element numbers: as defined for basic DDS.

COBOL mnemonics: as defined for basic DDS.

Synonyms: the alternative COBOL mnemonic(s) by which the same data element is known and used in various applications, modules, and programs.

COBOL pictures: as defined for basic DDS.

Originating system/subsystem/application's name: the system or application's name where the particular data elements were first defined.

Source: the division, department, shop, etc., that generated the particular data element(s).

Files: the files that contain the particular records that have the specific data elements residing in them.

Reports: the reports that display the particular data element(s).

Forms: the specific forms used in the enterprise that contain the particular data element(s).

Definitions: as defined for basic DDS.

Data structure: the rules and structure that the data must adhere to. For example, in the description of the data element SEX, the data structure might state "It must be a one-digit numeric code."

Values and description: as defined for basic DDS.

For an example of a one-page-per-data-element printout of an average DDS, see Figure 5.2.

Data Element Name:	CLIENT ID NUMBER
Data Element Number:	10031
COBOL Mnemonic:	ID NO.
Synonym:	CUSTOMER NO.
COBOL Picture:	X(13)
Originating System:	CLIENT INFORMATION DATA BASE (CIDB)
Source:	Accounting Department
Files:	Client Master, Cross Reference File
Reports:	All reports generated by CIDB
Forms:	None
Definition:	A number used to uniquely identify a client
Data Structure:	This code must be alpha-numeric and not more than thirteen positions

Value	Description
A	Commercial
B	Private
C	Unknown

Figure 5.2
Example of an AVERAGE DICTIONARY SYSTEM output.

5.2.3 Comprehensive/Sophisticated Data Dictionary System

A carefully planned, well-designed DDS at this level fully utilizes the capabilities of such a system. Whether it is a stand-alone or a dependent data dictionary that is an inherent part of a DBMS, it can take charge of an increasingly important corporate resource: its data. The comprehensive online DDS provides: accurate data definitions that in turn reduce programmers' coding time, automatic standards that ensure data uniformity and usability, and rules that enforce security.

In addition to the basic entities discussed previously, the

data descriptions stored in a comprehensive DDS may include some, most, or all of the following:

Source codes: the source codes, associated with COPY Library and data base descriptions, and maintained in appropriate form.

File definitions/descriptions: the definition/description of each file as it pertains to sequence, media, retention, backup, recording mode, programs using it, access requirements, and control and update procedures.

System descriptions: the detailed narrative of every one of the existing systems, including the conceptual or nontechnical description of each system's flow diagram, listing of the data base controls, and the functional or mechanical description of the modules and programs and their functions. Data in the latter description provides foundation for any future changes.

Record definitions/descriptions: the record size, block size, block format, number of formats, and update interval records in each file.

Specification data set: a repository of data element values to be used for input editing and output translation from a code to a detailed description.

Application-specification tables: the tables of specifications that reside in data sets and may be used by application programs to drive their own operation. Simply put, the tables contain specifications of data describing how they are used in application programs.

Object code procedures: the procedures for generating object codes.

Operational information: the description of storage media, backup requirements, restart and recovery procedures, and availability criteria of critical personnel.

Relationships: the associations between two or more data elements, as well as relationships between different types and structures of data (file to record to data element, for example) and between different types of processes (system to program or vice versa, for example). File/task relationships are also included.

Flow of data: the information about the flow of data across functions in the enterprise.

Conversion transactions: the definitions of conversion transactions that can be used in generating conventional file management utilities.

Updated conceptual and implementation views of data: the latest recorded version of these views. (This information should be available only to authorized staff.)

Listing of various levels of users: a record of users who are allowed to access a large portion of DDS and these users' functions and responsibilities. It is also a list of users who are authorized to access confidential data and update the DDS.

Glossary: Explanation of the terms peculiar to the industry in which the particular enterprise happens to be.

The additional capabilities provided by the comprehensive DDS may include some, most, or all of the following:

Data redundancy: providing fully documented information on data redundancy in online mode, and controlling future data redundancy.

Data analysis: giving information on the fundamental data structure of the enterprise, which then can be used by the data administrator for data analysis.

Functional analysis: providing information on how functions and events use particular data. By analyzing this information the DA can determine if the methods used are efficient.

Procedure for updating the DDS: detailing transaction procedure for adding, changing, or deleting any item or structure in the DDS. (This information should be available to the DA and certain users only.)

Collection and evaluation of performance statistics: collecting and reporting performance statistics on various applications as well as hardware, so that the DA can evaluate system performance.

Proposed change description: providing details on proposed change, as well as inconsistencies and possibly overlooked factors. This capability of DDS allows the data administrator to assess the possible impact of the change on other systems and various functional areas before the actual change is implemented. The assessment of the impact of change is then turned over to the systems analyst whose task is to modify part of a system. With this information he or she can prevent or at least lessen any side effects of the change.

Test and production programs control: providing control of test and production definitions of programs.

Consistency checks: performing consistency checks to ensure that the information the DDS contains is complete, accurate, and in the proper format. These validation procedures may be performed during input or when checking the correctness of the mapping between the updated version of the conceptual view and the implementation view of data.

Report generator: providing formatted reports that describe the contents of the DDS and their usage.

Program code generator: generating access or input/output modules for the processing units based on the stored information of the sequence of data use by processing units and the information on data structure.

Validation program generator: generating validation programs based on the stored validation rules.

Security enhancement: limiting access to sensitive data, definitions, and DDS functions to unauthorized users.

6

STEPS PRIOR TO BUILDING A DATA DICTIONARY SYSTEM

If a data dictionary system is to solve the problem of eliminating variations in the enterprise data that is shared and interchanged, and improve control and communications in all levels of company activity, it must be built on a sound basic structure. And to achieve this, certain steps must be taken; certain tasks must be performed *before* the actual building of the DDS is undertaken. The order in which these steps are to be followed, however, is dependent on how the DDS will be ultimately used. Specifically, whether it will be used for online access by applications software, or for data base maintenance and report generation only. Nonetheless, the quality of work at this stage will determine the integrity and functionality of the DDS. Consequently, every possible information about the enterprise data, which includes the distinct name, characteristics, description, attributes, and status (current or superseded), at this critical point must be identified and clearly defined.

Still, regardless of its ultimate usage, these procedures or steps apply whether a company opts for building an in-house data dictionary or purchasing a commercial DDS package, whether it is a stand-alone or a dependent DDS.

The six major steps in building a DDS that will respond to the enterprise's need for having complete control over their data resource follow.

Establishing data naming and definition standards/conventions: This includes standardization of data elements, data items, and data definition (DD) naming conventions, program naming conventions, and job name naming conventions, at minimum.

Establishing standard abbreviations and acronyms: This includes standardization of abbreviations and acronyms, as well as of establishing the rule to define a term the first time it is being used in programs, documentation, reports, etc.

Identifying and defining "base data" data elements: This includes the identification and definition of "product data" and the "division or department data" of the enterprise, both of which are essential for the company's existence.

Identifying and defining codes: This includes identification and definition of code types of data elements.

Identifying, defining, and standardizing input, output, update, and validation procedures: This includes identification, definition, and standardization of I/O, update and validation.

Identifying and defining data characteristics: This includes the identification and definition of the characteristics of data.

Because of the widespread confusion about definitions of data elements and data items, an explanation of these information entities is in order before showing one method that can be used for establishing data naming standards and conventions. In this book, data elements and data items are used according to the following definitions.

A **data element** is the smallest unit of information that identifies a specific data field in a record, data set/file, report, or form. In other words, the data element is the basic unit from which records, data sets/files, and data bases are built. And that is why uniformity through standardization is essential, why a data element *must* have a unique name to identify the name of the field such as, for example, CLIENT NAME, or PLACE OF BIRTH. Moreover, to establish true uniqueness, one must in the case of common names like ROBERT JONES, for example, use the middle initial. Thus, ROBERT J. JONES would satisfy this requirement.

Data element definition must be a clear and precise description of what a data element is and *not* what it does or what its purpose is. For example, if the definition of the data element SEX CODE says "This field (position 33) is to provide a basis for checking the validity of the insurance claim," that is wrong. It should state "This field (position 33) defines the sex of the insured client/dependent in the claim." Data element definitions include name, definition, synonyms, values, and description of different values for codes. Terms or symbols in the designation must also be understood. It should indicate, identify, describe, and quantify. Simply stated, it should tell how much, how many, how large, or how long in time or frequency.

Note: Unless or until a specific value or meaning is applied to the data element field, it remains meaningless. For example, the data element CLIENT NAME is unassigned until a specific value is given to the field.

A **data item** is the value or meaning applied to a specific data element field. Thus, as just stated, the data element CLIENT NAME has no value until a data item like UNIVERSAL PRODUCTS or JOHN L. MILLER is given to it. Similarly, the data element CREDIT LIMIT is unassigned until the data item, such as $1,000.00, is given to it. Another example may be found in a personnel system records where the data element PLACE OF BIRTH has no meaning until the data item of that particular field is defined, like CHICAGO, ILL. Data items may be names, acronyms (of variable length), codes (fixed length), or quantities.

6.1 ESTABLISHING DATA NAMING AND DEFINITION STANDARDS/CONVENTIONS

Since an important feature of the data dictionary is based upon the principle that synonyms may be used for unique data elements but homonyms may not, and that the same name may not be used for different data elements, a consistent and standardized approach to make-up a name, and defining data and related issues is imperative.

Quite often systems people as well as programmers make up data element names and definitions to satisfy their needs alone in whatever application they happen to be involved. And unless these same people thoroughly document such selections, if they leave during or after the system is developed (high mobility of systems and programming personnel is a well-known fact), the new staff will have to do the programming job all over again because of the many confusing, undefined data elements. Additionally, without established and documented standards, it is almost impossible to decipher abbreviations and acronyms written by a person no longer with the organization.

In a file system, especially one that evolved piecemeal—which is the case in most organizations—it is understandable when there are duplications of data elements, since traditionally a particular data element belongs to a particular application. It is also traditional that neither systems people nor programmers communicate very well with each other, and even less with non-DP users. Case in point is a well-known health care delivery system company. It was found—when management decided to complement their data base system with a DDS—that while in the Claims Processing Subsystem of their Medicaid Management Information System (MMIS) a numeric field data element was named CLAIM LIMIT, in the Provider Subsystem the same data element was named DOLLAR LIMIT. Further, the data element CENTRAL BILLING ADDRESS was found in a second file of the same system defined as LOCATION OF CENTRAL BILLING. In both of these examples the data elements were identical but named differently by two different programmers who worked side-by-side on the same MMIS, never thinking of communicating with each other. At another facility (an import company selling interior decorating novelties both wholesale and retail), a programmer coded the data element SALES TAX

58

SWITCH as SALES-SW, while another programmer coded it as TAX-SW.

The example on the following pages shows one possible (simple) way of establishing program naming conventions in the Front End and the Back End of a Management Information System and its various subsystems, as well as data definition (DD) naming and job names conventions.

SAMPLE APPLICATION

Lloyd S. Corporation
Management Information
System (MIS)

SYSTEM: MIS   REF:
                                     DATE:

A. PROGRAM NAMING CONVENTIONS

I. Front End

MISPAXXX
1. MISPA—Represents MANAGEMENT INFORMATION
   SYSTEM PROGRAM "A" SERIES.
2. XXX—Three-digit numeric ID.

      Example: MISPA∅∅3
              MISPA∅∅4 — SORT
              MISPA∅15
              MISPA∅18 — SORT

Note: Even numbers indicate internal sort or sort verb in use.

II. Back End

MISPBXXX
1. MISPB — Represents MANAGEMENT INFORMATION
      SYSTEM PROGRAM "B" SERIES.
2. XXX — Three-digit numeric ID.
    Example: MISPB∅21
          MISPB∅22 — SORT

III. Control Series

MISPCXXX
1. MISPC — Represents MANAGEMENT INFORMATION
      SYSTEM PROGRAM "C" SERIES.
2. XXX — Three-digit numeric ID.
    Example: MISPC∅22 — SORT
          MISPC∅23

IV. Financial Systems

MISPFXXX

V. Merchandising Systems

MISPMXXX

VI. Reference Systems

MISPRXXX

B. DATA DEFINITION (DD) NAMING CONVENTIONS

INPUT	OUTPUT
M—Management	M—Management
IS—Information System	IS—Information System
X—Series	X—Series
XX—Last two digits of program	XX—Last two digits of program
XX—Two digits (even)	XX—Two digits (odd)
Example: For program MISPA004	Example: For program MISPB021

C. JOBS NAMING CONVENTIONS

MISAJ03	Front End
MISAJ09	Front End
MISBJ21	Back End
MISBJ27	Back End
MISCJ22	Control Series
MISFJXX	Financial

D. EXECUTE JOBS NAMING CONVENTIONS

1. All MIS execute jobs in this facility have the following prefixes:

   a. MISRUNXX—MIS specifies that this job executes an MIS program. Run specifies that this is a production job. XX is the last two digits of the COBOL link module name.

   b. OSXXXX—where OS signifies that this is a compile of an OS module. The next XX indicate the origin of the program: for example, NJ for New Jersey, CA for California, FL for Florida, IL for Illinois. The last two digits refer to the relative position in the proces-

sing cycle. For example, OSNJ00 is the OS New
Jersey COBOL batch edit program.

c.   DYL180—since some report jobs use the DYL180
report features, the execute name reflects function
of the program, for example, NJORTP (New Jersey
Order Tape), CASLST (California Sales List), FLPO
(Florida Purchase Orders).

6.2 ESTABLISHING STANDARD
ABBREVIATIONS AND ACRONYMS

There is nothing quite as frustrating as reading a printout report,
a program listing, a file description, or a documentation that is
liberally sprinkled with abbreviations and acronyms but without
any explanation anywhere. More important, uncontrolled use of
abbreviations can lead to misunderstanding, duplications, and
problems.

The computer field abounds in acronyms that systems
people and programmers use constantly *without* knowing their
definitions. For example, the percentage of people at any random-
ly picked data processing facility who know the definition of
BASIC or HASP,* two commonly used acronyms, would be very
small indeed.

While the ideal situation would be to have uniform
standards for abbreviations and acronyms throughout the
country, the second best is for each DP facility to establish their
own standards. For example, it is essential that the address format of customers/clients, employees, vendors, etc., is standardized. The street address should always start with the street
number, followed by the street name, and then an abbreviation
such as

$$ST = Street$$
$$AVE = Avenue$$
$$RD = Road$$
$$BLVD = Boulevard$$

*BASIC = *Beginners All*-purpose *Symbolic Instruction Code.
HASP = *Houston Automatic Spooling* System.

$$CT \quad = \quad Court$$
$$HWY \quad = \quad Highway$$
$$PKWY \quad = \quad Parkway$$
$$PL \quad = \quad Place$$

Although these may seem too obvious, unless standardized, many of these abbreviations like HWY and PKWY tend to be interchanged with HWAY and PKWAY at the same facility.

6.3 IDENTIFYING AND DEFINING "BASE DATA" DATA ELEMENTS

Base data are essential corporate data and the foundation upon which the rest of the organization data are built. Base data exist on two levels. At the first level is the "product data" of the company. These are the data about merchandise, equipment, and service or a combination of product and service, as in the restaurant and hotel business or in the computer field. At the second level is the "division or department data." These might include existing and potential customer information, unique marketing strategy, and a particular proposal approach, if they are the Marketing Department's base data. Similarly, the Accounting Department and other departments, including the DP Department, have their own base data.

While some data may be peculiar to its "owner's department," as discussed in chapter 4, most departments' base data are interchangeable; that is, they need to be accessed by other departments. Thus, for example, the Costing Department needs to know what the Marketing Department proposed to a customer, and the Marketing Department needs to obtain the costing data (cost estimate) from the Costing Department. The Accounting Department needs data from the Payroll Department and the DP Department as to how long the project will take and how many staff at what cost will accomplish the project.

Obviously, it is very important that corporate base data are identified and defined. Base data at both levels can be determined by reviewing the work structure/work flow of the product of the company and the work flow of each particular department.

6.4 IDENTIFYING AND DEFINING CODES

To eliminate ambiguities that result in duplication of code types of data elements, codes have to be identified, defined, and standardized. Thus, if in one record the data element "CUSTOMER TYPE" is defined as "CUSTOMER TYPE CODE, COBOL Picture X(2), and value: '26' = retailer," in another record it cannot say "TYPE OF CUSTOMER, COBOL Picture X(2), and value '26' = one-store unit."

Similarly, values of codes have to be consistent with the name and definition of the data element. Thus, if the data element "EMPLOYEE STATUS CODE" definition states "It indicates whether the person is a full- or a part-time employee," and the values assigned are

FT	=	Full time
PT	=	Part time
LO	=	Laid off
FD	=	Fired

then the values and name are *not consistent* with the definition. In other words, close attention has to be given to consistency when describing codes and assigning values to them. Also, make sure that transaction codes for each application within the system are not only identified and defined but fully explained in the DDS, so that the system can enforce uniform definition of data elements.

For example, the transaction code in an Inventory Control system may say

"INV-CTRL-TRAN-CODE-'D' = Delete

ITEM CODE–15-position code of the particular stock item to be deleted.

ACTION–The particular stock item will be dropped from the Master File.

INV-CTRL-TRAN-CODE-'A' = Add

ACTION–Stock item will be added to the Master File exactly as specified.

INV-CTRL-TRAN-CODE-'C' = Change

STOCK ITEM CODE is required.

66

ACTION–Coded field will replace existing fields on the Inventory Master File. Blank field will be bypassed.''

Finally, if, for example, the SEX CODE in the Personnel System is using '1' for male and '2' for female, the Pension System cannot use 'M' for male and 'F' for female if a DDS has been implemented at the facility. The reason is that once a particular code is identified and defined in the DDS, the dictionary prohibits nonuniform definition or value of that data element.

6.5 IDENTIFYING, DEFINING, AND STANDARDIZING INPUT, UPDATE OUTPUT, AND VALIDATION PROCEDURES

Contents of a DDS can be input into the computer, updated, and output via a text-editing system, or input/output, and maintained online via specialized software. But unless the characteristics, input/output formats, data sorting, mode, and representation of these procedures are defined in detail, all the benefits of a DDS, in fact the whole purpose of a DDS, is nullified.

Definition of input and output procedures has a good deal of bearing on how data characteristics are defined. A particular data element could be defined as alpha or numeric, depending on output formats or data sorting procedures.

A DDS cannot perform consistency checks as to completeness, correctness, or proper cross-reference of the information it contains unless the *what* and *how* of each procedure is specified and standardized *prior* to the building of this system. Finally, the validation rules pertaining to each data element in the dictionary must be established, so that the DDS can provide one of its most important functions: validating all input data to meet the needs of quality control.

6.6 IDENTIFYING AND DEFINING DATA CHARACTERISTICS

The characteristics of a data element, i.e., whether it is alpha, such as "EMPLOYEE-LAST-NAME," Picture X(15), or numeric, such as "DATE-OF-EMPLOYMENT," Picture 9(6), and its relationship to those characteristics must be identified and defined before undertaking to develop a DDS. This is another measure for ensuring data integrity, representation, and security—especially in a distributed processing environment. A data dictionary thus developed ensures that the data sent at one point matches the characteristics of data received at the other end.

In a broad sense, under data characteristics the following may be included: size, classification, information, status, optional/mandatory presence, and usage. Data elements characteristics can also be based on the data derived from primary readings. Thus, one form of machine sensing can be translated into another. Analog readings, for example, can be converted to a binary form, or online data can be subjected to various forms of interpretation.

Perhaps at this point data characteristics should be clarified.

Data characteristics describe the relationship between the data processed and the entities, events, and properties that the data represent. Data characteristics are important for the proper representational function of the data, for example, natural language names, abbreviated names, codes, or special-use indicators as the name or substitute of the name of the data field on a record. Data characteristics define the relationship between the world and the machine-sensible records and files. It consists of names, codes, and numeric data. Thus, data characteristics can be defined, represented, and then formatted in data transmission.

Finally, it can be very helpful for systems people and programmers to include in the DDS a User's Glossary. This glossary could describe the non-DP users' jargon of the particular industry in which the enterprise is operating. Most industries such as the health field, restaurant field, or insurance field have their own unique terminology. The inclusion of the users' jargon in the DDS would serve not only the computer professionals (especially the newly hired ones) who may not be familiar with the "language" the company is using but new non-DP employees as well.

7

BUILDING
A DATA DICTIONARY
SYSTEM

Because data dictionary concepts—as in the case with data base concepts not too long ago—are far from being understood or appreciated, the design, development, and implementation of a data dictionary system should not be rushed. In other words, it is not enough to develop a plan, hire a data administrator, design a stand-alone or a dependent DDS (the latter to be added as an application to an existing data base or DBMS), transfer directly all the data definitions from the COBOL Copy Library (as well as all the information about files, programs, reports, etc., from the JCL/PROC Library, Application Programs Library, and LINK Library), and implement the DDS. This concept may be fine in theory but not in practice.

Unless the DDS is built slowly and deliberately using a

disciplined, step-by-step methodology, *plus maximum user involvement*, the project will run into problems such as the following:

1. Actual time, effort, and costs add up to much more than estimated.

2. Certain departments that "own" particular data are reluctant to share "their property." They are slow in submitting information on their data, their use, and definitions to the data administrator. They are disinclined to accept the standardization and stringent control that is necessary for the DDS (and the data administrator) to exercise over the creation and/or modification of data elements, files, and programs. These types of noncooperations can cause slippage in the schedule, effecting cost overruns.

3. When the DDS is operational, it is discovered that certain, essential user requirements have not been implemented.

4. A small but vocal group of users make it known that they are dissatisfied or even downright unhappy with the implemented DDS. They insist that a dictionary should contain, for example, an application-oriented definition of each data element, so as to reduce time in program preparation. However, if the same group would be involved intimately in the development of the DDS from the start, they would understand that formatting these definitions in a way that would satisfy the diverse users of the enterprise would require additional time and effort by the systems staff, thus further burdening an already strained project budget.

Make no mistake about it, building a data dictionary is not an easy task. It is a big project. And to ensure a successful end product, i.e., an efficient DDS that addresses and meets the users requirements, the project should be divided into subprojects or phases within a hierarchical structure. (See Table 7.1, Data Dictionary System Development Cycle.)

Table 7.1

Data Dictionary System Development Cycle

Phase I 6–10 Months	Phase II 3–6 Months	Phase III 6–10 Months	Phase IV 3–6 Months	Phase V 2–4 Months
Planning	*Requirements Definition*	*Designing*	*System Testing*	*Operations*
Long-range plan	Definition of all outputs	Logical design	Test specifications	Implementation of the tested system
Objectives	Deliverable	Physical design	Test description	Evaluation of the system in operation
Scope		Deliverable	Test procedures	Deliverable
Problem analysis			Forms	
Cost justification			Controls	
Identifying, defining, and standardizing all corporate base data			Equipment	
"Learning curve"			Manpower	
Deliverable			Data	
			Deliverable	

7.1 PHASE I—PLANNING

Because sound, careful planning is imperative in a system development cycle, this phase should be given 6–10 months in the project's time schedule.

The planning phase consists of the following:

1. Long-range plan
2. Objectives
3. Scope
4. Problem analysis
5. Cost justification
6. Identifying, defining, and standardizing corporate base data
7. "Learning curve"
8. Deliverable

7.1.1 Long-Range Plan

Establish a long-range plan that is pragmatic as well as flexible. And, equally important, secure commitment from top management to support the project through its development cycle. Being an overview of the whole project, the long-range plan defines the goal for the dictionary, the resources needed to accomplish the goal, the subproject activities, and the approximate time allowed for each of the subproject/phase activities. There also should be a strategy to mitigate the possible affects of the DDS upon various departments, especially the data processing department, where the impact of such a system will be felt the most.

7.1.2 Objectives

Define the primary and secondary goals of the proposed system. The most obvious objectives of a DDS, as stated before, are the centralizing of the corporate data resource and the cross-referencing, verifying, updating, and retrieving data about data in a fully documented online mode. Secondary objectives may include the ability to define modules, programs, and systems and the mappings between programs and systems; the ability to interface to

DBMS (if there is one or more); the ability to generate COBOL descriptions into a source program library; the ability to generate job control language (JCL); the ability to control the Production Libraries (JCL/PROC Lib, Application Program Lib, COBOL Copy Lib, and LINK Lib); the ability to generate documentation for statistical and functional analyses; and the ability to enforce security measures.

Except for the basic or primary objectives, the goals defined will mirror the particular environment in which the DDS will be set up and, of course, the resources available for the project.

7.1.3 Scope

Define the size and degree of sophistication of the proposed system, as well as the type of features that would be most useful in the particular facility where the project is being considered.

7.1.4 Problem Analysis

Define and analyze the possible problems that the project might encounter, and establish contingency plans to solve them or at least to mitigate them. Of course, it must also be considered that the stated problems may never arise, while other, quite different problems may rear up.

7.1.5 Cost Justification

Cost-justify the project by pointing out to management what would interest them the most in the short- and long-range benefits of a DDS. This would include the control and enhanced security of both automated and nonautomated corporate data resources and their usage through a centralized dictionary under the strict supervision of a data administrator.

7.1.6 Identifying, Defining, and Standardizing Corporate Base Data

Because this is a critical step, it has been discussed in detail in Chapter 4.

7.1.7 "Learning Curve"

People need to become used to the idea of sharing data and of having centralized control over the definitions and usage of data elements and programming methods, to mention a few things that can be upsetting to the staff who have been used to doing "their own thing" more or less. Consequently, establish maximum "learning curve" time for the staff of various departments.

7.1.8 Deliverable

Write a summary of each subphase to be submitted to top management. This deliverable must be approved and signed off by *top management* before the next phase can commence.

7.2 PHASE II—REQUIREMENTS DEFINITION

Depending on the size and complexity of the planned dictionary, this phase should be allotted 3–6 months. At this stage of the project development, all outputs that reflect not only the users' requirements but also the way the data are being used are defined.

The requirements definition phase consists of the following:

1. Definition of all outputs
2. Deliverable

7.2.1 Outputs

The outputs may consist of some or all of the following:

1. An inventory of accurate and timely information on the corporate data and their usage in departments, as well as in programs/modules, and their locations in files/segments, records, reports, etc.
2. Detailed definitions of unique data elements and their full range of attributes and interrelationships.
3. File definitions/descriptions.

4. DBMS, data base(s), network, and/or conventional file systems descriptions, as well as descriptions of change control at all levels.

5. Record definitions/descriptions.

6. Object code procedures.

7. Operational information.

8. Proposed change descriptions and impact analysis on how the change would affect different areas in the computer system as well as in the functional areas.

9. COBOL descriptions into a source program library.

10. JCL generation.

11. Listing of various levels of users.

12. A glossary that includes not only DP terminology but the particular terms of the industry in which the system is being developed.

13. Dynamically allocated time-limited passwords to users.

14. Log file report that shows who and when made an inquiry into sensitive information that resides in the DDS.

7.2.2 Deliverable

Write a description of each output. The end product must be approved and signed off by the *users* before the next phase of the development cycle can commence.

7.3 PHASE III—DESIGNING

This phase should be given 6–10 months in the time scheduling of the activities.

The designing phase consists of the following:

1. Logical design
2. Physical design
3. Deliverable

7.3.1 Logical Design

Design all data, i.e., records, files [such as VSAM (Virtual Storage Access Method) to gain indexed-sequential access to variable-length records], reports, etc., *from the output*, to address and meet user requirements. This is a blueprint for structured coding.

7.3.2 Physical Design

Design features for restart, backup, security, etc.

7.3.3 Deliverable

Write a definitive summary of both the logical and the physical design activities. This deliverable must be approved and signed off by *DP Management* before the next phase can commence.

7.4 COMMERCIAL SOFTWARE PACKAGES

Of course, you can take the other route and buy field-tested commercial software packages. By tying together two or more available packages, the time for this phase can be cut in half. More important, taking this route can mean substantial cost saving. The reason for this can be found in the great number of commercial system and utility software packages that are being offered. The competition is keen, and consequently the quality is high and the prices are reasonable. And, while the costs of in-house "start-from-scratch" system and program developments are spiraling, the prices of available software packages are becoming more attractive.

For example, there are many excellent mini to large computer-based data base system packages available that have a history of reliability, cost effectiveness, and vendor support. This might be an option for a DP facility that decides to establish a stand-alone DDS. If the decision is to build the DDS inhouse, either as a stand-alone system or as a dependent system, i.e., an integral part of an existing data base or DBMS, many first-rate products in the area of system resource optimization, system-related data management, and program development are being marketed. These packages are effective in aiding the systems staff, in shortening the design phase, and in reducing the development costs.

The following are just a few samples of commercial system and program software packages that are on the market.

7.4.1 Source Program Management

The most significant features of commercially available source program management packages follow:

- Security controls that stop updates to the wrong library, stop unauthorized updates, and supervise simultaneous updatings.

- Complete modules that may be inserted, replaced, or deleted.

- Measures that check modifications for errors.

- Features that generate job streams automatically.

- Highly compressed modes that provide impressive disk economy.

7.4.2 Online Business Terms Dictionary Systems

- Vocabulary files of any industry's specialized terminology or jargon may be built.

- Terms and meanings unique to a particular business may be entered and retrieved.

7.4.3 Sort/Merge Utilities

- Sort time may be reduced by 30 to 35%

- Disk space may be used efficiently without JCL changes.

7.4.4 Program and Data Generators

- COBOL programs may be generated from nonprogrammers' statements.

- Machine-efficient and documented COBOL programs may be produced from problem-oriented specifications.

- Program preparation and execution time may be substantially reduced.

7.4.5 Program Test/Debug Packages

- These packages may be utilized to debug, test, and efficiently use COBOL source code.
- Adaptable test data may be generated for COBOL programs.
- A drastic reduction in paging may be achieved.

7.4.6 Report Generators

- Formatted reports are created from computer files.
- Manipulation of complex files as well as interfacing with data base systems for sophisticated information retrieval are provided.

7.4.7 Job/Procedures Handlers

- Repetitive data sets, programs, and control language statements are isolated. These then can be referenced from all related job streams and procedures.
- The user is allowed to nest control procedures. This facilitates the initiation of a single JCL change and its reflection throughout the whole system.
- A single procedure is stored and maintained. This procedure then can be expanded at execution time into multiple job streams.
- The user is allowed to control dynamically at execution time the sequence in which steps within a job are to be executed.

7.5 PHASE IV—SYSTEM TESTING

This phase should be given 3–6 months.

The system testing phase consists of the following:

1. Test specifications

2. Test description
3. Test procedures
4. Forms
5. Controls
6. Equipment
7. Manpower
8. Deliverable

7.5.1 Test Specifications

For each system testing, fill out the following test specification items completely and accurately.

- System/Module
- Title of test specification
- Test ID number
- Date
- Prepared by
- Approved by
- File and/or program needed
- Form(s)
- Dependency (of one file to another)
- Input
- Procedure (how to simulate the test)
- Expected results
- Actual results
- Actual cycle time

7.5.2 Test Description

Write a brief narrative, describing each test.

7.5.3 Test Procedures

Write a concise description of the specific test procedures that are performed by each of the following departments.

- Systems and Programming Department
- DP Operations
- User Department
- Data Administrator Controls

7.5.4 Forms

> Input test data
> File creation
> Maintenance

7.5.5 Controls

Write a concise description of the specific control measures that are performed by the following departments.

> User Department
> Data Administrator Controls

7.5.6 Equipment

Describe briefly how the equipment is performing in the system testing.

7.5.7 Manpower

Describe briefly the manpower that is being used for system testing in the following departments, as well as the specific measures taken by the data administrator to monitor the manpower resource.

> Systems and Programming Department
> DP Operations
> User Department
> Data Administrator Controls

80

7.5.8 Deliverable

Since the purpose of the system testing is to ensure that all the system's ingredients work together well, DP management should not approve and sign off on the deliverable, unless all components on the System Check List have been checked off by the appropriate parties, thus indicating that all activities have been performed satisfactorily.

7.6 PHASE V — OPERATIONS

This phase should be allotted 2–4 months.

The operation phase consists of the following:

1. Implementing the tested system.
2. Evaluating the system in operation.
3. Deliverable.

7.6.1 Implementing the Tested System

Test the complete system after the testing phase is finished to ensure that all modifications have been taken care of satisfactorily. Then implement the system in phases by introducing one section of DDS at a time. Because 'going live' is crucial, it is advisable to give each section time to be accepted before introducing the next section.

7.6.2 Evaluating the System in Operation

Evaluating the DDS after a few days of its live running ensures that problems are discovered and corrected before the system goes into maintenance.

NOTE: To avoid later problems, ensure that the corrections are thoroughly tested by the same criteria as used in system testing.

7.6.3 Deliverable

Complete documentation of the new system. Since the operational DDS controls the data resources of the enterprise, it is imperative that the final documentation of this system is approved and signed off by ALL LEVELS OF MANAGEMENT.

If the five-phase system development cycle has been adhered to, no major problems should arise with the implemented dictionary. Of course, as with any new system, minor modifications and changes are to be expected.

8

OVERVIEW
OF AN OPERATING
DATA DICTIONARY SYSTEM

8.1 BACKGROUND

Because the emphasis of this book is on providing practical information that can be used readily by the reader and because an actual sample application is the best tool to effect that, this chapter presents the description of an operating DDS.

For the past few years, development efforts to fully integrate data dictionaries with data base systems have been regarded as innovative. But the Computer Systems and Services Department of Pacific Gas and Electric Company (PG&E) of San Francisco, in 1970 under Manager Honien Liu, built a corporate data bank system comprised of several subsystems, including a DDS to support a comprehensive information system. Thus,

PG&E has been using a data base system with a fully integrated DDS for a decade.

Before presenting an overview of this particular data base system and a detailed description of the operational DDS, which PG&E calls Data Bank Administration & Control Subsystem (DBACS), a bit of background of this company is appropriate.

PG&E provides service to 5.7 million customers in 48 northern and central California counties. Its electric operations include nuclear, steam, hydro, geothermal, and gas turbine generating units and approximately 100,000 miles of power transmission and distribution lines. The gas operations involve transmission of natural gas from Canada as well as from Texas and from gas wells in California. The gas from these varied sources is distributed to industrial, commercial, and domestic customers in 37 counties. This utility company has about 130 business offices and scores of service centers throughout their 13 operating divisions. In short, PG&E is a large company with diverse activities that involve some 25,000 employees and lots of data.

8.1.1 Overview of the Corporate Data Bank System

This system is comprised of the following components (see Exhibit 8.1):

> *The Data Manager Subsystem (DMS):* in conjunction with the operating system—controls the flow of data between core memory and disk or tape storage. Through its data formatting ability, it stores data in the most efficient physical form and presents it to application programs and the Data Base Retrieval programs in a form suitable for their use. This provides considerable program independence from data storage structure. Further, it allows changes in the method of physical storage, and even permits improvements to the DMS without causing rework of application programs. The DMS also provides teleprocessing security, based on operator, terminal, and transaction authority tables.
>
> *The Table Manager Subsystem (TMS):* controls the transfer of application tables from disk to core and carries out specified table searching. The techniques utilized

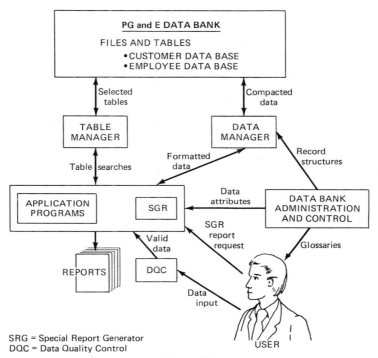

Figure 8.1
Courtesy PG&E

here provide efficient processing and core utilization. To minimize program maintenance, there is extensive use of tables in program design.

The Data Bank Administration and Control Subsystem (DBACS): provides a computer file of data descriptions. The DBACS, serving as the reservoir of information about data, is the primary data administration tool. It provides data definitions for the user glossary, data attributes for the COBOL Data Divisions, and record structure information for the DMS.

Data Retrieval Software: includes a Special Report Generator (SRG) for overnight preparation of user-specified ad hoc reports and an online general retrieval subsystem that allows direct access to online data bases.

Data Quality Control (DQC): (a table-driven validation

package) provides the capability for maintaining a historical record of rejected data and the facilities for re-entry of corrections.

8.1.2 Narrative Description of DBACS

The following pages offer the Table of Contents and an *abbreviated* account of the operating DBACS data dictionary system, which was developed inhouse at PG&E. The example includes an overview of the system and its use and a definition of DBACS facilities and input transactions.

SAMPLE APPLICATION

Pacific Gas & Electric Company Data Bank Administration and Control Subsystem (DBACS)

TABLE OF CONTENTS

Through the courtesy of PG&E San Francisco, California

Common Data Element Definition
File and Record Facility
Control Stages
Changing Control Stage
File Definition
Table Definition
System Glossary Definition
Record Definition
Glossary Control
Data Divisions

Section 3

Input Transactions

SECTION I   INTRODUCTION

One very important Company resource is data. As with all Company resources, we need to use and manage data in an efficient and effective manner. Our Data Bank's integrated set of computer files contains billions of characters of business data that represent the plans, results, status, characteristics, and effects of the Company's operations. These data must be available to all authorized information users within the Company. Also, since data are a Company resource, we need the ability for many users to share the data so that we minimize duplicating data and facilities.

       To help meet these needs, Computer Systems and Services Department has developed the Data Bank Administrative and Control Subsystem (DBACS).

What Does DBACS Do?

One of the functions of the Computer Systems and Services Department is to develop, design, and program management-authorized, computer-based information systems, new and modified. DBACS is a tool to help us do this job by reducing duplication of data descriptions, by storing those standardized descriptions in one central location, by reducing the overall programming effort by providing complete descriptive information at the outset, and by encouraging the sharing of data between subsystems.

From a single definition, DBACS produces data descriptions in meaningful business terms for the user, in programmer terms for the programmer, and in technical terms for the Data Management System. This contributes to the Department's goal of reducing the cost of maintaining comprehensive, coordinated information systems.

DBACS and System Development

DBACS is an integral part of System Development. Its use in systems development is as follows:

1. Standard input transaction forms are provided to define data elements during External Design and to define further those data elements during Internal Design.
2. Standard input transaction forms are provided to define and describe files during Internal Design.
3. A procedure is established to aid in combining the data elements into records during Internal Design.
4. A procedure is established to aid programmers in updating all the computer-related information during the Program and Test step.

DBACS and Systems Maintenance

DBACS is also an integral part of Systems Maintenance. It supports the concept of ensuring the operational readiness of production systems while, at the same time, allowing test modifications during Service Request processing. Its use in systems maintenance is as follows:

1. Operational versions of computer-related information placed in production libraries ensure availability at time of production job failures.
2. A procedure is established to create test versions of computer-related information in test libraries to allow updating and testing outside of the production environment.

Through the courtesy of PG&E

SECTION 2 DBACS FACILITIES

Common Data Element Facility

The function of the Common Data Element (CDE) facility is to maintain centrally common descriptive information about data elements. The common information consists only of information that does not change when a data element is used in different files.

Information for a data element is provided at three levels:

GENERAL-The basic description of a data element without regard to its usage in a particular system or file.

SYSTEM-Describes the usage of a data element within a system.

FILE-Describes the file-related usage and attributes.

Each common data element has the following information: NAME, DEFINITION, ALTERNATE NAME(S), MAXIMUM LENGTH, NUMERIC/NON-NUMERIC designation and COBOL NAME BASE, available for use in any system via a simple reference. The reference consists of the common data element number generated by DBACS and the version, either test or operational. Information received from a common data element may not be overridden although it may be supplemented at the system level (within the CDE facility) or at the file level (within the record facility).

The CDE facility maintains the following independent versions of a common data element:

TEST-For use in a test environment. All information may be modified.

OPERATIONAL-For use in a production environment. All information is protected and may not be modified.

RETIRED-An operational version that has been removed from general use by the Administration and Control group. All information is protected and may not be modified or used.

Common Data Element Definition

The Common Data Element Description (40 transaction) is used to define a common data element.

90

Is the Common Data Element Currently Defined in DBACS? Prior to defining a common data element, be certain that it is not defined in DBACS already. To assist you, a microfiche report — "COMMON DATA ELEMENT INDEX" — is available. The report is in alphabetical sequence by name and each entry indicates the common data element number. The number may be used to scan another microfiche report "COMMON DATA ELEMENT DICTIONARY," which is in sequence by common data element number. Each entry contains all information about the common data element. If the data element does exist, it may be used in your system. Information related to your particular system may be entered at this time if needed. The method will be described later.

Common Data Element Number Assignment Common data element numbers are automatically assigned by DBACS when new elements are added. To make use of this facility, enter a unique number for each common data element being added in one day. This, in combination with your initials, will ensure a unique identity while the transactions are entering the system. Once a common data element number has been assigned, it must be used for all modification transactions.

The Data Bank Administrative Unit will preassign blocks of common data element numbers on request. When this option is used, all 40 transactions initially describing the common data elements must have a number in the COMMON DATA ELEMENT NUMBER field.

Creation of a Test Version of a Common Data Element Definition Creation of a test version is automatic in the common data element facility each time transactions are entered. No other action is required.

Describing a Common Data Element The NAME of a common data element (format 10) may be up to 60 characters in length and should be as meaningful as possible. Place keywords at the beginning of the name to provide optimum identification. Avoid use of abbreviations wherever possible.

The DEFINITION of a common data element (formats 11 through 22) should be no more than a straightforward statement of what the data element is. No reference may be made to its usage in a particular system — this is user information and will be described later. Spacing within the body of the definition may be provided by skipping the use of one or more formats. Use standard hyphenation when continuing a word from one format to the next. The definition will appear

Through the courtesy of PG&E

in the COMMON DATE ELEMENT REGISTER exactly as it is entered on the transaction.

Two ALTERNATE NAMES (formats 31, 32) may optionally be entered for each common data element. The rules for the format of the alternate names are the same as those stated for NAME.

The length and numeric/nonnumeric designation (format 40) of the common data element should always be specified at the time the data element is created.

The COBOL NAME BASE may optionally be entered at the time the common data element is created or later. Although space is provided for 26 characters, try to use no more than 15 characters, so that ample room will remain for the use of COBOL ELEMENT SUF-FIXES.

Common Data Element Register Each time transactions are entered for a common data element a Common Data Element Register will be delivered to you on the following workday. All information that has been entered on the 40 and 41 transactions appears on this report.

Supplementing a Common Data Element with User Information User information is related to the specific use of a common data element in a system. This information will appear in all glossaries for that system which use the common data element. When supplementing a common data element with user information, the SYSTEM CODE must always be specified on the transaction. Format 40 may not be used to enter user information.

Changing a Common Data Element Description Some common data elements are designated as corporate data elements by Administration and Control group and no modification to these data elements is permitted without authorization from that group.

When changing the description of a common data element, enter only the information that is to be changed. Do not reenter all the description previously entered. If user information is being changed, SYSTEM CODE must be specified on the transaction, and format 40 may not be used.

Adding COBOL Names to Common Data Elements If COBOL NAME BASE was not specified for common data elements when they were created, the 41 transaction may be used to enter this information. Although space is provided for 26 characters, try to use no more than 15 characters, so that ample room will remain for the use of COBOL ELEMENT SUFFIXES.

Through the courtesy of PG&E

How to Request Operational Status When you are satisfied that your common data element definitions are correct, prepare an Operational Status Assignment Request (OSAR).

How to Request Copies of Common Data Element Register Whenever you enter the 40 or 41 transaction, a Common Data Element Register is automatically generated by DBACS and delivered to you on the next workday. If you require additional copies (up to four) or want reports for which no transactions were entered, use Administrative Requests (02 transaction). Enter your initials, common data element number, number of copies and version (if other than test).

Deleting Common Data Elements A test version of a common data element may be deleted at any time by entering an 02 transaction with your initials, common data element number, and "Y" in delete test version.

Retiring Common Data Elements Operational versions of common data elements may be retired only by the Administration and Control group. Follow normal Control Unit procedures for retirement of operational systems/jobs.

File and Record Facility

The function of the file and record facility is to maintain descriptive information such as file descriptions and usages, logical record structure, references to common data elements, and definitions of unique data elements. This descriptive information is used by DBACS to generate descriptors for use by design teams, programmers, and user departments.

Generally, control in the file and record facility is by File-id, a reference that identifies file type, file number, and system. A list of current numbers is located in the Data Bank Administrative Unit's office

There are two levels of file definition in DBACS.

1. Record—All data elements in the logical record are defined.
2. Usage—No data elements are defined but it has the same logical structure as a given record to which it is assigned as a subordinate.

Through the courtesy of PG&E

Control Stages*

Six Control Stages provide the Data Bank Administrative Unit with a means for controlling the DBACS working environment and administering the proper procedures during the various stages of a project.

A Control Stage identifies the kind of work that members of a project are doing. The Control Stages follow:

1. Design
2. Development
3. Development modification
4. Operational
5. Operational modification
6. Delete

Figure 1 shows that as work progresses in a project, changes to the DBACS descriptions require a change from one stage to another.

Design Stage File description transactions submitted to the Data Bank Administrative Unit for all a project's new File-ids are automatically assigned to the Design Stage.

DBACS checks the information entered on the transactions to verify that current standards are followed.

As shown in Figure 8.1, once Design work is completed, the File-id must be assigned to Development Modification Stage for testing. No descriptors are generated into test libraries during Design Control Stage.

Development Stage Any new programming and testing of a project that is not operational must have the File-id(s) assigned to the Development Stage when going into a production environment. When a File-id is assigned to this stage, DBACS places certain processing requirements (data divisions, file directories, etc.) into production libraries. No modification to any of the DBACS descriptions are allowed when a File-id is in Development Stage. This safeguards the DBACS descriptions so that members of a project work only with "correct" information and need not be concerned with it changing.

---

*The use of Control Stages is scheduled to be phased out, being replaced by version control as in the common data element facility.

Through the courtesy of PG&E

94

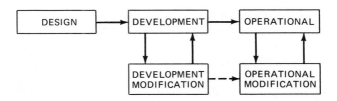

Figure 8.1 Control Stages.

As shown in Figure 8.1, a File-id may be moved to either Development Modification or Operational Control Stage.

Development Modification Stage File-ids must be assigned to this stage whenever modifications to the DBACS descriptions (in the Development Stage) are required. When a File-id is assigned to this stage, DBACS places the modified processing requirements into test libraries.

After testing of the modifications has been completed, place the File-id back into Development Stage where the new descriptions will once again be secure.

DBACS checks the information entered on the transactions to verify that current standards are followed.

Figure 8.1 shows that a File-id may be moved to Development and then back to Development Modification. This loop can be made as many times as necessary. Figure 8.1 also shows that a File-id can be moved to the Operational Modification Stage. This is indicated by a dotted line because such a move can be made only under special circumstances that will be discussed shortly.

Operational Stage All File-ids for operational systems must be assigned to this stage. Place the File-id (DBACS descriptions) into this stage after all testing is completed and when it is necessary to secure all the DBACS descriptions. No modifications of the DBACS descriptions are allowed when a File-id is in Operational Stage. This safeguards the DBACS descriptions so that the operational jobs run only with correct descriptive information. As shown in Figure 8.1, a File-id may be moved to Operational Modification Stage (for maintenance).

Operational Modification Stage File-ids must be assigned to this stage whenever an operational system is in a maintenance environment. When a File-id is assigned to this stage, DBACS places the modified processing requirements into test libraries.

Through the courtesy of PG&E

95

Moving the File-id back to Operational Stage must be coordinated with the Data Bank Administrative Unit because installing changes to an operational system must be checked out thoroughly.

Delete Stage This stage is unique in that it allows a File-id (DBACS descriptions) to be deleted from the DBACS files. The associated information on the Data Division, File Directory, Record Structure Table, Model Record and Data Quality Control libraries will also be removed.

The information in the DBACS masterfile will be maintained for 2 months before it is removed. During the 2 months, it is possible to reinstate the File-id and all its associated information by placing it back into a Modification Stage.

Development Modification Stage to Operational Modification Stage If a project is going into an operational environment (not to be confused with Operational Stage) and some changes to the DBACS descriptions are pending, the File-id(s) can be moved from Development Modification Stage to Operational Modification Stage (which, in effect, puts the project in a maintenance environment).

Changing Control Stage

To move a File-id (DBACS descriptions) from one Control Stage to another, submit a "Control Stage Assignment Request."

There are times when it is advantageous to submit more than one Control Stage Assignment Request a day for a single File-id:

1. A File-id may be moved from Development Modification Stage to Development and back to Development Modification. The first move would put all pending transactions into the Development Stage; the second move allows a new set of modifications to be entered.

2. A File-id may be moved from Operational Modification to Operational and back to Operational Modification.

3. A File-id may be moved from Development Modification to Development and then to Operational.

4. A File-id may be moved from Development to Development Modification and then to Operational Modification.

Through the courtesy of PG&E

If the "selection of pending transactions" option is checked, the Control Stage will not change.

Disposition of Transaction A transaction entered into DBACS is assigned one of three dispositions.

1. Posted—The transaction was processed and the information is current in the permanent DBACS masterfile.

2. Error—The transaction was not processed because of a compatibility or logic error. An error report is returned to the person who submitted the transaction.

3. Suspended—The transaction was processed but the information is in a "tentative" version of the DBACS masterfile. Transactions that are not in error but are submitted for File-ids in Development Modification or Operational Modification are automatically suspended. All suspended transactions are listed on a report in the Data Bank Administrative Unit's office.

Selection of Pending Transactions There are times when it is advantageous to leave some transactions "suspended"; i.e., in a Modification Stage. To request that transactions remain suspended, check the box on the "Control Stage Assignment Request." Consider using the option in the following situations:

1. When a number of changes have been submitted for a File-id, it is often necessary to make some of the changes operational and leave others in a modification stage. By checking the box on the form and discussing the situation with the Data Bank Administrative Unit, you can select the transactions to be posted (or exclude the transactions to remain suspended).

2. Changes that have been submitted are sometimes found to be unnecessary. By checking the box on the form and discussing the situation with the Data Bank Administrative Unit, you can delete the unwanted transactions.

Changing to Development or Operational Stage When changing to Development or Operational Stage, it is important that all reports and computer data be up to date. No reports are delivered

Through the courtesy of PG&E

automatically, but the Data Bank Administrative Unit will perform the following:

1. Generate the following reports, if applicable, and put copies in the folders in the file cabinets:

    File Register
    Working Glossary
    Data Division Report
    Data Element Register
    Record Structure Table Report
    DQC Process Report

2. Remove all previous reports from folders in the file cabinets.

3. Coordinate the movement of the new computer information into production libraries, if applicable.

File Definition*

The Device Characteristics (11 transaction), File Characteristics (12 transaction), File Description (13 transaction), File Characteristics Extension (17 transaction) and, optionally, File Definition Worksheet (100 transaction) must be used to adequately define a file.

FILE-ID is a required entry on all file definition forms (RECORD on the 100 transaction). FILE-ID consists of three parts: "file type" (first character), "file number" (characters 2–4), and "system code" (character 5–6).

FILE TYPE may be one of the three characters:

    F—master and transaction files
    R—report files
    W—work area Data Division
    (M, L, and S are reserved to maintain existing files only.)

FILE NUMBER is numeric and unique within the system code.

SYSTEM CODE must be alphabetic and must correspond to the system code specified in Table T244.

*This is an abbreviated version of File Definition.
Through the courtesy of PG&E

Table Definition

All tables must be defined in DBACS. There are two types (data quality control and dynamic) and the requirements for each are discussed separately.

Data Quality Control Tables There are three data quality control tables associated with transaction files that make use of the Data Quality Control facility. A fourth (optional) table, "ERROR CODE," is a dynamic table and must be defined as such in DBACS.

Each data quality control Table-ID must be described in DBACS on a File Description (13 transaction).

Dynamic Tables A File Characteristics (12 transaction) and a File Description (13 transaction) must be entered into DBACS to define dynamic Table-ids. If a data division is required, a Data Division Options (18 transaction) must also be entered.

System Glossary Definition

System glossaries serve as the reservoir of all known data elements in a system.

File Description A File Description (13 transaction) must be completed and entered into DBACS to describe a system glossary.

Data Element Definition All the data elements that will be used in a system must be identified and defined in the system glossary. Some data elements may be currently defined in the Common Data Element facility and may be used in your system glossary with or without minor additions of system-related information. Other data elements may be defined in the Common Data Element facility on the Common Data Element Description (40 transaction).

Including a Common Data Element in a System Glossary Use Glossary Generation and Control (60 transaction) to include common data elements in your system glossary. Glossary control information may also be entered on this transaction at the same time that common data elements are being selected.

If you wish to have user information added to any common data elements in your system glossary, it may be entered at this time.

Working Glossary Report A Working Glossary is automatically generated each time you enter transactions related to a system glossary. All the information about each data element is contained in this report. For ease in maintaining your system glossary, the source

Through the courtesy of PG&E

99

of information is indicated under the heading "SOURCE." If all the information is unique to the system glossary, no source is indicated.

> GEN—extracted from the common data element facility.
>
> SYS—user (system information extracted from the common data element facility).
>
> FILE—unique information entered on a 54 transaction.

If you wish to have a data glossary in user format, prepare a REPORT REQUEST specifying the sequence and the number of copies required.

If you need extra copies of the Working Glossary report, specify the number required (up to four) on a Report Request.

Changing a System Glossary Entry Before preparing transactions to change an entry in a system glossary, determine the source as specified in the Working Glossary. If the source indicates that the information was extracted from the common data element facility, see "COMMON DATA ELEMENT DEFINITION—Changing a Common Data Element Description" in this section of the manual. If the information is unique to the system glossary, see "RECORD DEFINITION—Changing Unique Data Elements in a Record" in this section of the manual.

Deleting a System Glossary Entry Use a Data Glossary Generation and Control to remove a data element from a system glossary.

Record Definition*

Once the data elements have been defined in a system glossary, the elements may be organized into logical records.

54 Transaction and Unique Data Elements in a Record The Data Element Description (54 transaction) should be used to define any data elements that are unique to a record.

Procedure to Create Records All common data elements used in a system are defined in the system glossary. Either the 54 transaction or EDP Record Information (55 transaction) may be used

---

*Both the Record Definition and the following Glossary Control sections are abbreviated versions of the original text.

Through the courtesy of PG&E

to create a record from the common data element facility. The 54 transaction should be used if definitions unique to a record are to appear in the user's data glossary or if glossary control information is required.

1. Write the File-id for the record on each transaction and enter the common data element number.

2. Create any elements (and fill out 54 transactions) that are necessary to complete the record definition such as
   a. control elements (e.g., increment maps, segment counters, etc.).
   b. increment group definitions.
   c. processing control elements (e.g., counters, dates, programming keys, etc.).
   d. FILLERS—these may be defined on a 55 transaction, format 10 only. The COBOL name "FILLER" will be generated by the system.

3. Organize the elements (and transactions) into the logical record order and assign the sequence number within the record.

4. Complete the EDP information for each data element. Make use of defaults wherever possible.

Glossary Control

Use the Data Glossary Generation and Control (60 transaction) to make changes to the content or sequence of the user's data glossary. Only the glossary is changed, not the record or file structure.

   Glossary Sequencing Three basic ways of sequencing elements in a data glossary are available to meet the different requirements of the users:

1. Logical Order—The elements are sequenced by SEQUENCE NUMBER WITHIN THE RECORD. Periods printed to the left of the name reflect the hierarchy of the elements. To delete elements (or to restore previously defined elements that once were deleted), code the "Show on Glossary" field on the 60 transaction. Then, enter a Report Request to generate a "new" data glossary.

Through the courtesy of PG&E

2. Data Name Order—Elements are in alphabetical order by name. To delete elements (or to restore previously defined data elements that once were deleted), code the "Show on Glossary" field on the 60 transaction. Then, enter a Report Request to generate a "new" data glossary.

3. Glossary Sequence Number Order—The sequence of the elements is by "Sequence Number Within Glossary." If any two (or more) elements have the same sequence number, those elements are further sequenced by name. To change the sequence of elements, specify the new sequence numbers. Then, enter a Report Request to generate a "new" data glossary.

All three types of the data glossary may be generated at the same time.

Data Divisions

A COBOL data division is one of the major output reports from DBACS for use during the EDP Design and Program and Test steps of Project Development. Some of the information from the 54 transaction and 55 transaction is used to create a data division. Specifications on the 18 transaction and the organization of elements into logical record order also contribute to creating a data division. COBOL Coding Standards must be considered when building data divisions.

Data Divisions and the 54 Transaction, 55 Transaction Certain fields of these transactions that correspond to the Level Number, COBOL Data Name and five clauses of the Data Description Entry of a Data Division are outlined below.

SECTION III INPUT TRANSACTIONS

This section describes each of the input transaction forms for three of the DBACS facilities: Common Data Element Definition, File Definition, and Record Definition.

Descriptive information (name, definition, and use) and characteristics (maximum length, input editing, permissible values, and

Through the courtesy of PG&E

default values) are specified for the individual data elements of each transaction.

Data Division Entry		Field(s) on the Transactions
1. Level Number	54/55	Level Number
2. COBOL Data Name	54/55	COBOL Name Base (Note 1)
	54/55	COBOL Name Suffix
3. Picture Clause	54/55	Used for Arithmetic Calculations (Note 1)
	54/55	Decimal Places (Note 1)
	55	Edit Picture
4. Occurs Clause	54/55	Maximum Times Group or Data Occurs
5. Usage Clause	54/55	Numeric Data Representation
6. Redefines Clause	55	Redefines
7. Value Clause	54/55	Standard Initial Value
	55	Value

Notes: 1. These fields are predefined for common data elements and may not be overridden.

9

EFFECTIVE USE
OF DATA DICTIONARY
IN SYSTEM DEVELOPMENT

A data dictionary can be of particular value to systems analysts/designers in the three phases of system development: (1) analysis, (2) design, and (3) implementation.

9.1 ANALYSIS PHASE

Since in this phase both general and specific analyses of current data resources are required to establish a sound basis for the proposed new/modified system, as well as to ensure (as much as possible) that the system will realize its full potential, a DDS can be an excellent device to assist the analyst in accomplishing these requirements.

Specifically, verification of the basic data in existing systems can be done by a simple inquiry of the DDS. Moreover, the dictionary can identify the use of data as it relates to the functions (processes) of the enterprise, and it can produce a description of data requirements in terms of an entity/attribute/relationship data (conceptual) model. This model, being an accurate account of the organization's functions, can then be used for reference by the analyst, as the new/modified system is being developed to respond to a real-world situation.

By calling upon a DDS to perform some of its previously discussed functions, the systems analyst can ease the task load and reduce development time.

In brief, since analysis is generally described as the phase in which problems are investigated and defined and solutions are recommended, the DDS can be an effective instrument for providing essential data (including nonmechanized data) to the analyst. Having these data then enables the analyst to present an accurate and comprehensive statement of the problem, indicate possible solutions, and provide the key for an orderly change control.

9.2 DESIGN PHASE

Within the framework of the DDS-created data model, the systems analyst/designer can analyze user requirements and verify that the proposed system will meet these demands.

Because at this juncture there is always a possibility that management—after another review of justification for the undertaking—will postpone or "kill" the project, normally only a general or overview design of the system is prepared. While management is reviewing the project's justification—usually a lengthy process—the systems analyst can once again utilize the dictionary by determining, via data supplied by DDS, if any existing systems will need modification because of planned links to the proposed system.

If management decision is affirmative, the analyst can proceed with the detailed design of the system. Specifically, by means of the DDS, the analyst can add details of the proposed system's processing and data structure to the data model and construct an implementation model that meets the requirements specified in the data model.

9.3 IMPLEMENTATION PHASE

The implementation model should contain all possible information about data elements and the programs that use them: validation rules for correctness, and conformity to the rules of usage; frequency of use of the applications processed; and the accessing paths that the applications follow. Further, to allow test data to be produced by DDS, the permissible ranges of values for data elements should also be included in this model. In addition, detailed description of data structures is a desirable inclusion, since such information at this level allows DDS to generate data description to be incorporated in the host language and the conversational language programs.

During input to the implementation model, the systems analyst can call upon the dictionary to perform consistency checks to ensure that the new data is complete and correctly formatted. Moreover, further validation by DDS can confirm proper mapping between the data model and the implementation model.

Finally, since the DDS—monitored by the Data Administrator—contains the information as to who may have access to specific data sets, records, segments, etc., another of its functions should be access control. This can be accomplished by channeling all queries or references from application programs through the DDS.

The following pages show the existing Veterans Administration Data Dictionary (VADD) that is being used to manage system development and support VA personnel in the design and maintenance of many of VA's computer systems, including the current Target System. The dictionary was developed inhouse at the Veterans Administration Office of Data Management & Telecommunications, Washington, D.C. However, VADD is not utilized by the new/upgraded Target System (a sophisticated, integrated, online "User System") Data Base Administrator. This is because the new Target System is a highly complex network of interactive data bases and because it operates on a different vendor's hardware than the majority of VA systems. Consequently, a dictionary, which will be one of the subsystems of the new Target System, is under development at the VA facility.

      To understand the need for another dictionary, the example includes an overview of the Target System, the new system configuration, geographical network configuration, system software, and major software "extensions." The last section includes the dictionary that is being tested. This dictionary will be used by the Data Base Administrator to manage development of and assure control of Honeywell's DM-IV DBMS. This is followed by a Table of Contents of the VADD Handbook and a narrative of VADD.

Target System
Veterans Administration

TARGET — A USER'S SYSTEM

From its inception, the Target System has been designed and developed to serve the end users of the system, those regional office personnel who deal directly with the Veteran and who are responsible for development, of claims and subsequent awards. The present system has been described as technically limited, labor intensive, and paper bound. To overcome these inefficiencies, an online inquiry and claims processing system was essential. In the familiar terminology of government systems procurement and development, the two major considerations are cost savings and service benefits. In the area of

Through the courtesy of VA Office of Data Management & Telecommunications, Washington, D.C.

cost savings, it has been proven in numerous studies that the system will substantially reduce the personnel required to process claims at the regional offices, offsetting increased ADP employment by a substantial margin. A net recurring savings of approximately $137 million has been projected for the life cycle of the system. The efficiency provided by an online system that provides accurate, timely information in seconds, as opposed to the cumbersome and time-consuming process involving the current system, streamlines operations at the regional offices to such a degree that the substantial employment reductions are feasible. The substantial savings in processing times and increased accuracy of information will provide a number of benefits to veterans who file claims.

Since virtually all claims for benefits follow a basic pattern of development and authorization, regional office claims processing personnel have been organized according to a unit concept, under which an individual claim remains functionally and organizationally within a unit. The Target System supports this functional and organizational unit concept and, in fact, was designed to facilitate it.

In support of this function and organization, the Target System incorporates inquiry and claims actions by a series of commands. Online inquiry to the Beneficiary Identification and Records Locator System (BIRLS), located in Austin, Texas, and interfaced with the three regional processing centers, allows the claims clerks to determine the veteran's or dependent's eligibility for benefits based on service records and other information. The BIRLS system also assigns claims folder numbers and establishes folder location. It allows information retrieval by name, claim number, service number, or social security number. The BIRLS record can also be updated online. Master record inquiry is accomplished via interface between the regional processing centers and the central system data base located in Hines, Ill., a suburb of Chicago. This type of inquiry provides all information available on prior claims by a veteran or dependent. The master record inquiry provides all relevant service dependency and eligibility data available on the veteran or dependent.

Two other forms of inquiry are related to a Pending Issue File, which is related to the stages of claims development. When a claims clerk receives an initial or supplementary claim from a veteran, the claim is established on the Pending Issue File, which is basically a work-in-process file maintained at the regional processing center. This

Through the courtesy of VA Office of Data Management & Telecommunications, Washington, D.C.

file contains all pending claim records until they have passed through the five stages of development. At the point of final authorization, a transaction is generated and transmitted to the central processing system for update of the master record and generation of a payment request to the U.S. Treasury Department. The Pending Issue File inquiry displays the claims record as it exists in the various stages of development. The status inquiry provides information as to the stage of development and the physical location within the regional office of the claim. These inquiries enable benefits counselors or other employees to provide instantaneous information to the veteran as to the status of a claim and what documents or information are required to complete his or her claim.

Within the claims development process, the various stages are completed through a series of commands. Such commands provide for computer-generated letters, initiate notice of death processing, and record all data entered by the user.

Miscellaneous functions and commands in the Target environment allow changes to the Hines CP&E master file and BIRLS file, records statistics on data entries and claims disposition, effect CP&E disallowances, facilitate internal claims, routing, post cycle rejects, and provide user, file, and jurisdictional security with related security logs and violation reports.

SYSTEM CONFIGURATION

The Target System is a complex, interactive network of terminals, minicomputers, modems, and mainframe processors that support those claims processing functions described above. Basically, the major components of the system are the Target Central System (TCS), the three Regional Data Processing Centers (RDPCs), the Beneficiary Identification and Records Locator System (BIRLS), and the Terminal System (TS).

A. Target Central System

The Target Central System, which houses the Target Central System data base for Compensation, Pension, and Education records (approximately 14 million records), consists of a dual Processor 66/60

Through the courtesy of VA Office of Data Management & Telecommunications, Washington, D.C.

that supports not only data base activities but also the batch processing workload of the Interim Target Central System (ITCS) — the current Compensation, Pension, and Education Systems that has been converted from IBM COBOL/ALC to ANS COBOL 74 for processing on Honeywell. The TCS is linked to each of the three Regional Data Processing Centers by a Datanet 6600 Computer, which handles communication between the TCS and each RDPC.

B. RDPC Systems

The three Regional Data Processing Centers consist of a dual Processor 66/80. The processors are crossbarred, with the capability of each utilizing all system resources available. Linked to the TCS for master record inquiry, the RDPCs are also linked to the Beneficiary Identification and Records Locator System through Datanet 6600 computers. These computers also handle communications between regional offices and the RDPCs. The RDPC system is basically a work control mechanism, with conversational interaction between the Terminal System and application modules resident at the RDPC. Each RDPC maintains a Pending Issue data base for award actions in process of development or adjudication. The three RDPCs in Chicago, Los Angeles, and Philadelphia support the regional offices in appropriate geographical areas. The workload for each is projected as reasonably balanced; each will handle approximately 30 to 35% of the national workload.

C. BIRLS

The Beneficiary Identification and Records Locator System (BIRLS) located at the Austin, Texas VA Data Processing Center, is an integral part of the Target System. The equipment utilized for BIRLS processing is a triplex IBM 360/65 environment under ASP/OS. The communications software is INTERCOMM. The BIRLS data base consists of approximately 35 million records containing locator and service information.

     The Target System interface operates with Honeywell Information Systems' VA FEP/TS Protocol communication procedures in full duplex synchronous operation with ASC II Transmission Code. As a result of the Target communications interface, we have a

Through the courtesy of VA Office of Data Management & Telecommunications, Washington, D.C.

Protocol Conversion System (PCS) in order to have communications between BIRLS and the Target System.

The PCS is a microprocessor based communication adaptor designed to interface the BIRLS data base and the Target Network. The connection to BIRLS is accomplished by means of twelve serial ports of the Comten Front End Processor, while the connection to the Target Network is via six high-speed synchronous communications lines (two per RDPC). This PCS assumes an active communications role during its initialization phase in order to establish connections with the BIRLS and Target Systems, and thereafter becomes a relatively passive element performing code speed and protocol conversion necessary to support message flow between the BIRLS and Target Systems. The PCS is comprised of three identical subsystems, each of which is used to support the connection of four (4) BIRLS COMTEN ports to two (2) communications lines in support of a single Target Network Processor mode.

D. The Terminal System

The Terminal System encompasses by far the greatest volume of specific pieces of equipment. At a typical regional office, the basic components of the system consist of a specified number of video display terminals (VDTs) and printers that are linked to 7765 Controllers. Each Controller can handle eight terminals or printers. The Controller handles, through firmware, the basic function keys and associated control functions. Up to eight Controllers can be linked to a Level 6 minicomputer, which is in VA terminology a "Level 2" device. The "Level 2" devices handle such functions as screen mapping, downline loading, Supervisory Terminal Operator logic, and unique software requirements peculiar to regional offices. Depending on the amount of equipment located at the regional office, there may be an additional Level 6 minicomputer ("Level 3" in VA terminology) to service as a concentrator for multiple "Level 2" devices.

E. Hardware

The total contracted equipment at the TCS, the three RDPCs, and the regional offices is as follows:

    HOST SYSTEMS: 8 Level 66s

Through the courtesy of VA Office of Data Management & Telecommunications, Washington, D.C.

(RDPCs & TCS)	12 Datanets
	150 Disk Drives
	56 Tape Drives
REGIONAL OFFICES:	100 Level 6s
	405 Terminal Controllers
	2600 VDT's
	800 Printers

This is the basic equipment specified in the contract. However, the contract also contains an augmentation clause which provides for purchase of additional equipment in amounts up to one-third of the purchase price of the equipment originally specified in the contract. In some areas, the VA has already exercised the augmentation clause to contract for additional core, 6250 BPI tape drives, and other equipment. Future Target requirements will also be examined for potential utilization of augmentation funds.

GEOGRAPHICAL NETWORK CONFIGURATION

Trunk Network: The trunk network connects each RDPC with the TCS and BIRLS. There are multiple circuits between each RDPC, TCS, and BIRLS. The circuits in the trunk network will be full duplex, synchronous point-to-point circuits. The circuits that terminate at the RDPC and TCS interface with the technical control center located at these installations.

Optimized Star Networks: The circuits required for each optimized star network have a line speed of 9600 BPS. They are full duplex, synchronous point-to-point circuits. The communications circuits for each optimized star network interface at the technical control center located at each RDPC. As you can see, each RDPC is the maintainer station for regional offices within a specified geographical region.

Mirror Image Concept: The concept of three Regional Data Processing Centers provides for economical and efficient distribution

Through the courtesy of VA Office of Data Management & Telecommunications, Washington, D.C.

of workload. The three regions operate essentially on a mirror image concept during the online day. The hardware configurations, system software, and applications software will be as identical as is possible. The VA is currently planning to implement a system release concept with applications software changes. This concept is necessary to manage effectively the complex network development as well as to maintain mirror image software at all three RDPCs.

The magnitude of the system from an equipment standpoint is impressive. It is most certainly the largest ADP project the VA has ever attempted, both from the point of view of the scope of the implementation and the point of view of its impact upon nationwide VA operations.

SYSTEM SOFTWARE

To support the Target network, the VA made the decision early after contract award to upgrade the data management software offered under the contract (IDS-I/TDS) to Honeywell's DM-IV. There were a number of reasons for this upgrade beyond the desire to implement a state of the art environment. One of the major reasons was the fact that DM-IV supports the current (U.S.) Federal Standard for COBOL. Benefits to the use of COBOL-74 include upward compatibility for future Federal COBOL standards, uniformity for future maintenance and development, as well as relatively simplified training approaches.

Conversion of the online portion of the system from a CICS/TOTAL data base environment was much less complex with DM-IV than would have been the case with IDS-I/TDS, because of interprogram communication problems. The modularized nature of the Prototype online system was much more readily converted utilizing DM-IV, and maintainability of the system should be greatly facilitated.

Still other factors in the decision to utilize DM-IV involved the stated objective of Honeywell to maintain it as the state of the art data management system, the support of ASCII character code, and the compatibility with draft specifications for data base management standards of the CODASYL Group.

Virtually all the system software initially provided by Honeywell has undergone extensive modification to meet the needs of the

Through the courtesy of VA Office of Data Management & Telecommunications, Washington, D.C.

complex network that is necessary for Target operations. The basic GCOS software is the only major system software that has remained essentially unchanged during the implementation effort. Many of the changes made to the basic packages installed will be described later. The basic system was functional both in a batch and a stand-alone on-line environment. What remained was to tailor the system to VA network requirements and the operational needs of the regional offices.

MAJOR SOFTWARE EXTENSIONS

Networking: One of the major software extensions developed for the VA was a networking capacity. Since the Target System was designed with numerous computer-to-computer interfaces, it was necessary to develop methods of communications between the host processors, the TCS, and RDPCs. The distributed processing and data base philosophy of the system is based on the concept of a dominant host computer system that communicates with subordinate and remote host computer systems. Modifications to DM-IV and GRTS II have been developed and networking is now in production on a nationwide basis.

Pipelining: The pipelining feature, which allows a balance of message traffic over more than one physical data communications line, was integrated into GRTS II software. The feature enables the direction of messages, or even parts thereof, across different physical lines and their reconstruction in proper sequence at the receiving end. This feature has been installed nationwide between the RDPCs, TCS, and BIRLS.

Level 6 Queuing: Because of the necessity in regional office operations for certain types of printed records pertaining to awards and authorization, it was necessary to develop a mechanism where the printed record could be obtained without suspending transaction processor activity at the host printer should printers be unavilable at the terminal site. Queuing allows for timely printing on an as available basis by queuing delivered messages until such time as a device becomes available. This feature is currently installed at our Terminal System sites.

Training Mode: A nationwide terminal network requires a sophisticated training mechanism. When eventually implemented na-

Through the courtesy of VA Office of Data Management & Telecommunications, Washington, D.C.

tionwide, a total of 10,000 to 12,000 regional offices' personnel must be trained for terminal system operations. The training mode feature allows the Supervisory Terminal Operator at each regional office to designate whether a terminal will be placed in production mode or in training mode. This feature actually accesses a separate area of the data base. All training transactions generated are designated by an indicator that triggers DM-IV to access only the specified area of the data base allocated to training mode. Production records in the data base are not accessible. Otherwise, the terminal commands, screens, and processing in the training mode are identical to the production versions. The feature allows, then, for training in a mode identical to production processing without endangering production data. The training mode facility has been implemented.

Variable Field Protect: Because of the variety of screens available for inquiry and for update purposes, the VA required a feature that would prohibit entry or change of data to a screen field that is not authorized for update with a particular command. Although applications software ignores extraneous data for a particular command, a feature was required that would prevent the terminal operator from entering data in a protected field and assuming that this data would be normally processed. The variable field protect feature is an enhancement to the 7765 Controller that will dynamically protect and unprotect fields as required by a particular command. This feature is currently installed.

Downline Loading: Because of the large number of remote sites, a feature was necessary that would enable transmission of Level 6 software such as new or modified VDT screens from the host computer. The feature will also allow for loading of software from the dominant to the subordinate host. This software could be both applications releases and systems software releases. Since the major development activity for the Target System will take place in Chicago, this feature will be invaluable for maintaining software integrity according to the mirror image concept associated with the RDPCs. The facility also ensures integrity of Level 6 software at all regional offices. The downline loading facility is currently being tested.

Data Element Dictionary (DED): This product is currently being tested. It will be used by the data base administration function to manage development of and assure control of DM-IV application data bases. In the future, the DED will be an invaluable tool for

Through the courtesy of VA Office of Data Management & Telecommunications, Washington, D.C.

standardizing and enhancing data base organization and structure.

Terminal Simulator: This feature of DM-IV TP software allows for the simulation of terminal activity in a number of ways. The simulator has potential in several areas of application software testing and in audit activities. This software is currently being tested.

NOTE: Since a new Data Element Dictionary, a subsystem of the substantially upgraded Target System, is being developed, only Chapter 1 (Objectives of VA Data Dictionary, and System Overview) of the existing VA dictionary is presented on the following pages.

CHAPTER 1—PART A.
OBJECTIVES OF THE VA
DATA DICTIONARY

It is the policy of the Veterans Administration that data is a resource which must be managed and controlled. The immediate goal of the VA is to make maximum use of the existing data resource without restricting it. The quantity of data maintained by the VA is so great that the only way to manage and control it is to list what data exists and to describe it. An effective tool for the listing and describing data is a Data Dictionary/Directory. The VA Data Dictionary is an inventory of all VA automated data processing applications and descriptions of their component data elements (i.e., fields), master files and reports. This comprehensive and detailed inventory of data elements provides a structure for the control of changes to the current data resource and serves as the key first step towards future standardization efforts. The objectives of the VA Data Dictionary are:

- To standardize data elements, through a data inventory, by first identifying and then isolating those data elements with common definitions and attributes.

- To identify and eliminate and/or prevent redundancy and inconsistencies in data elements used within VA ADP applications.

- To provide detailed documentation of data elements, to insure that all pertinent facts about the elements are communicated directly and concisely to both ADP and non-ADP management.

Through the courtesy of VA Office of Data Management & Telecommunications, Washington, D.C.

- To aid VA personnel in determining the impact of proposed and/or approved changes in data elements by identifying the programs, master files and reports in which the data elements appear.

- To support VA personnel engaged in designing, maintaining and managing automated systems by providing easily comprehensive reports describing the VA data resource.

CHAPTER 1— PART B.
SYSTEM OVERVIEW

Identification

1. The Veterans Administration Data Dictionary (VADD), designed and developed by the Data Element Management Staff of the Veterans Administration, was installed July 15, 1976. This sytem is the responsibility of the Privacy and Data Administration Division (334), and the point of contact is the Data Element Management Staff, phone (202) 389-3034.

Scope

2. The VA Data Dictionary is an information tool by which the Veterans Administration intends to manage and control the resource called data. This information tool is an automated, central collection point for a current and complete description of all VA data elements. In addition to this dictionary feature, the system is also a data directory in that data elements are linked to application systems, user programs, master files and reports. The purpose of the Dictionary is described in the section called "Functional Characteristics".

Operating Requirements

3. The VA Data Dictionary is installed on VA's IBM Series 360/40 computer, running under OS/MFT Release 21.8. The system requires 90K bytes of main storage, a single 2314 disk (to be used for inter-

Through the courtesy of VA Office of Data Management & Telecommunications, Washington, D.C.

mediate word files), two tape drives (three may be used as an alternative to disk for purposes of spooling output) and a printer. If required, the VA uses, hardware permitting, a Xerox 1200 off-line printing system.

4. The dictionary programs are written in ANS COBOL.

5. Data element master records, master file and report records are stored on magnetic tape. The system is to run in a batch mode with update and report processing to occur a minimum of twice a week. It should be noted that frequent update of the master file will provide users with the most current, up-to-date information on data elements within their application(s).

6. Input in the Data Dictionary system is accomplished through key-entry equipment using seven different transaction formats.

7. Storage of the Master Files on tapes makes it very conducive to distribution of these files to the various VA Data Processing Centers throughout the United States. This will permit each Data Processing Center any portion of the Dictionary that is in current demand.

Functional Characteristics

8. The VA Data Dictionary generates several reports on the data element contents of VA applications. Three distinct report types are produced: "Element Description Report", "Master File Report", and "Reports" report. These reports are generated when: (1) bi-weekly, changes occur to information content of a data element, master file, or report, or (2) semi-annually, the entire contents of the Data Dictionary is printed.

9. The primary report generated by the VA Data Dictionary is an Element Description Report (COIN DDM 4) which lists all data elements within a VA application. Some information provided includes: permuted word (key identifier of the data element); element name; Source Responsibility (organization that controls or manages a VA Program Application); narrative description of the element and its related values, user programs and VA departments that use the data element.

10. As stated previously, the VA Data Dictionary links data elements to application master files and reports. The "Master File Description Report" (COIN DDM 5) identifies, by application system, all data elements stored within a master file in its proper sequence. An "Element

Through the courtesy of VA Office of Data Management & Telecommunications, Washington, D.C.

Structure Report" (COIN DDM 6) identifies, for each report generated by an application system, all data elements used in the creation of the report.

11. A by-product of this dictionary is the "Permuted Word" Report. A "Permuted Word" Report lists all VA data elements, in Permuted Word sequence, and the application system that uses the data element. For a brief explanation, this provides a means of cross-referencing data elements common to multiple applications.

12. The update program generates separate lists, by application system, for all accepted or rejected transactions. In addition, a statistical summary report lists, by application system, individual totals for the number of elements, master files and reports contained in the VA Data Dictionary Master File for an application, in addition to other miscellaneous statistical data.

13. The VA Data Dictionary provides an ad hoc query facility through the use of optional reports. These reports, run on an IBM Series 360 computer, or other compatible computer hardware, consist of specific application requests or partial reports about: (1) a specific data element or (2) the contents of a specific application master file, or (3) the data elements used in the construction of each report.

14. The system does not have an RPG capability nor provide any interactive activity, special utilities or interfaces with any other system. However, at a later time, certain information may be extracted from the system and used as input to a Data Base Management System.

15. The total number of data elements in the VA is approximately 82,000 elements. As of September 1976, there exist 359 application systems in the VA. This amount can easily be handled by the VA Data Dictionary.

Security

16. Procedures have been established for the development of and access to the VA Data Dictionary. Access is available to all authorized personnel in the Veterans Administration. Tape copies of the master file are available to all DPC's for query and optional reports at a user's request. Since the dictionary is a "hard-copy" version, limitation of access is not intended to be restrictive; since at the present time, it is not intended to be a data base system.

Through the courtesy of VA Office of Data Management & Telecommunications, Washington, D.C.

17. All input documents are submitted through the Privacy and Data Administration Division for review and analysis. Computer-generated reports are distributed to authorized personnel according to established procedures.

Integrity

18. Procedures have been established to insure integrity of data to be submitted to and processed by the VA Data Dictionary. These include various circulars and Data Dictionary Handbook. Continued usage of the dictionary by the responsible sources of information will assist in the integrity of the dictionary.
19. The VA Data Dictionary edits not only for validity but completeness of data submitted for processing. Free-formatted area is not edited. Back-up to the master file is provided through retention of father and grandfather master files and transaction tapes.

Data Characteristics

20. The VA Data Dictionary Master File, stored on magnetic tape, is organized by sequence number within transaction code within Permuted word within application acronym. The Record Length is 125 positions, blocked 8. There are seven multiple fixed length master records that contain: (1) specific information on a data element (such as name, description, values); (2) element content of an application's master files and (3) data elements that are used in the creation of application system reports. A Summary record follows each Application System storing necessary statistical data.
21. Data to be entered into the VA Data Dictionary System initially is obtained from existing system documentation found in manuals, circulars and directives, or through the expertise of various individuals. Appropriate systems personnel at a VA Data Processing Center (DPC) may provide data such as application program names, master files and reports content. This data gathering and preparation can be phased in at different time periods. That is, data element name and description will establish a data element on the master file with additional information to be provided at a later time.
22. The organization responsible for management and control over a VA application (the "Responsible Source") will designate certain per-

Through the courtesy of VA Office of Data Management & Telecommunications, Washington, D.C.

sonnel to prepare input data to the VA Data Dictionary. These people, commonly referred to as "Information Specialists", should be familiar with and knowledgeable of the information contents of their application systems.

23. Enhancements to the basic VA Data Dictionary will begin approximately 6 months after the initial installation (not meaning the total implementation of all application systems).

Users

24. The VA Data Dictionary is a useful information tool to be used by VA, and not limited to a specific application or geographical area. Because of the layman's language description and definition of data elements the dictionary may be utilized by ADP oriented as well as non-ADP oriented management and staff. As a result, the dictionary may be used as a reference point for communication among management, "Responsible Source", users, programmers and analysts. It also will be used as the basic ingredient in formalizing a data base system.

Through the courtesy of VA Office of Data Management & Telecommunications, Washington, D.C.

10

ROLE OF DATA DICTIONARY SYSTEM IN MAINTENANCE CYCLE

It is a well-known fact that even the best designed and most comprehensively tested computer system is subject to changes almost as soon as it is implemented. The changes may come about because of requests from dissatisfied users (who did not really know what they wanted, but who now are not satisfied with the delivered system) or because of errors missed in testing and now discovered. Or perhaps because of certain characteristics required by local conditions at different installations, in case of a distributed data processing system.

Necessary changes in the delivered system may also be the result of incomplete requirement analysis, inaccurate functional specifications, errors in design, errors in coding (which surprisingly is not as frequent an occurrence as in design), or insuffi-

125

cient testing. Insofar as the last item is concerned, if test plans have not been formulated and specific test data not defined during the design phase, or if one of the three distinct testing operations—module testing, integration testing, and systems testing—has been rushed or left out, or dumped into one operation, the result is the same: inadequate testing. This then produces an immediate need for modification of the operating system.

Whatever the reason for system or application changes, maintenance costs invariably eclipse development costs during the life of the system. And it is in maintenance—an important if pedestrian phase of the systems development cycle—that the data dictionary proves to be a very useful tool in dealing with the countless maintenance problems and in keeping the costs to minimum. Specifically, the DDS can be used in the following:

1. Assessing the impact of changes on programs or modules.
2. Maintaining change control in test and production.
3. Providing audit trails of the changes.
4. Documenting the reason for changes.
5. Providing version control.
6. Reducing the amount of tedious work for maintenance programmers.

Details of how data dictionary services may be used to aid in performing these maintenance tasks are discussed in the following paragraphs.

10.1 ASSESSING THE IMPACT OF CHANGES

Through the use of the dictionary, the project manager can be supplied with information as to how often a data type is used, what programs or modules use it, and how it is presented to those programs or modules. This sort of information can be invaluable to the data administrator and/or the project leader in assessing the impact of changes to the data on other programs or modules, and the cost/benefit of any proposed change. Similarly, the DDS can be used to facilitate the task of analyzing the impact of changing applications by cross-referencing computer steps, procedures, programs, and data sets using "where used" indexes.

10.2   MAINTAINING CHANGE CONTROL IN TEST AND PRODUCTION

By assuring that changes are reflected in all affected COPY Lib members and file documentation (the latter according to documentation standards) and that file changes are reflected in creation of or maintenance to COPY members and data elements, the DDS provides change control in test and production.

10.3   PROVIDING AUDIT TRAILS OF THE CHANGES

By documenting the changes as they occur, the dictionary provides audit trails of changes in systems and applications.

10.4   DOCUMENTING THE REASON FOR CHANGES

Whenever changes are proposed in a system or application, the DDS can be used to document the reason for the changes, thus providing future reference.

10.5   PROVIDING VERSION CONTROL

Proliferation of different versions of a system because of subsequent changes can be avoided by recording in the dictionary—during the specifications stage of systems development—the various procedures for reporting, testing, and correcting errors before the changes are distributed. This method will ensure that all users (and installations) use the same (latest) version of the system.

10.6   REDUCING WORK FOR
MAINTENANCE PROGRAMMERS

The DDS can be a great help to the maintenance programmers by automatically generating file descriptions through COPYs into their programs. The COPY facility cuts down the total amount of coding required. And having the codes copied rather than re-entered eliminates not only the tedium of writing a lot of codes but reduces the number of errors as well.

In addition, by identifying, describing, and cross-referencing application codes used by Job Control Language (JCL), the dictionary can be used to research an application; that is, the DDS can show each application in its executable form, with called procedures inserted in proper sequence. Also, the data dictionary can be used to describe briefly the function(s) of each application code.

Finally, if there is any question about the availability of certain data because of privacy or other constraints, the dictionary can provide that information to the maintenance programmer, thus further aiding him or her in the task at hand.

The following pages provide a sample application of a data dictionary that is heavily used in the maintenance phase of the systems development cycle, as well as the operations processing. The material is taken from the in-house developed Data Dictionary/Directory (DD/D) of the San Francisco based Del Monte Corporation.

Del Monte's DP operating system consist of an IBM 3031, MVS/SE (Multiple Virtual System/System Extension), Cincom's Total DBMS, and ENVIRON/1 (Cincom's Communications Monitor), and MARK IV.

Del Monte's DD/D is a stand-alone system. However, it feeds on COPY Library and JCL Call Deck (tape images of all Production JCL in the system).

The types of application programming maintenance problems that the Del Monte's DD/D helps in solving are the following:

1. To find location of particular data elements and their usage.
2. To use it as a check list for verifying correctness of changes in the system.

128

3. In new applications development, to research and review the existing data elements, their usage, and their relationships.

4. In operations processing, to check in the indexed tables (built into the DD/D) where and what to change.

Del Monte's JCL Dictionary System and Data Dictionary System

TABLE OF CONTENTS

10.14.2   **Data Dictionary System**

10.14.2.1   DESCRIPTIVE OVERVIEW
    .2   DICTIONARY REPORT OUTPUT
    .3   MANUAL INPUT

10.14.1 JCL DICTIONARY SYSTEM

10.14.1.1 Purpose

To produce an accurate, timely, and complete dictionary that identifies, describes, and cross references Application codes used by Job Control Language (JCL). Application codes used by non-computer jobs are not included.

This dictionary can then be used to:

A. *Research an Application.* Each Application is shown in its executable form, with called procedures inserted in proper sequence. Symbolic, refer-back, and refer-forward references are resolved.

Each Application code is briefly described.

B. *Assess the impact of changing an Application.* Complete cross referencing is provided between computer steps, procedures, programs, and data sets using "where used" indices.

C. *Separately identify and describe the installation's report output.* Computer reports are listed and described in name, title, responsibility code, and special form sequences.

D. *Control the production procedure library.* Procedures not used by Job Control Language, and procedures used, but not found on the Procedure Library, are listed.

10.14.1.2 Descriptive Overview

A. These codes are identified, described, and cross referenced:

Code	Description	Cross Referenced
Application	X	
Process	X	
Job	X	
Step	X	X

Through the courtesy of Del Monte Corp.

Table continued

Code	Description	Cross Referenced
Procedure step	X	X
Procedure end	X	
Program	X	X
Data Set	X	X

B. Job Control Language and the DMC Procedure Library are used to identify and cross reference Application codes.

C. Application authors, in response to a pre-printed turn-around form, provide one-line code descriptions (typically a data set or program title). Temporary and dummy data sets are system-defined, and descriptions are automatically posted to codes that are used more than once. Thus, for data sets, descriptions are required only for new non-temporary sets.

D. Six dictionary reports are provided in three dictionary books for Application reference and cross reference.

10.14.1.3 Dictionary Report Output

Two Procedure Library control reports (Exhibits 7, 8), filed separately in the Computer Center, identify library add and delete candidates (members used, but not found, and members not used).

Two reference books and one cross reference book are filed at the Remotes service counter. They are used separately, or in combination, to research an Application and to assess the impact of changing an Application (via "where used" indices).

Reference Books

Exhibit

1. Book 1. DCBBR103, *Job Control Language Narrative.*

Each Application is listed in executable form, with data set and program references and symbolics resolved. Each Application code is titled.

Through the courtesy of Del Monte Corp.

2. Book 2.   DCBBR121,   *Report Data Set Listing — Responsibility Code.*
Reports are indexed by user department.

3.   DCBBR161,   *Report Data Set Listing — Title*
Reports are indexed by subject matter.

4.   DCBBR171,   *Report Data Listing — Number*
Reports are indexed by report number.

5.   DCBBR181,   *Report Data Set Listing — Form*
Reports are indexed by special form number.

6. Book 3.   DCBBR191,   *Cross Reference Listing.*
   a. *Procedures Section.* Job-steps using Procedures list.
   b. *Data Set Section.* Job-step-programs using data set list. Job-step-program creating the data set is asterisked.
   c. *Program Section.* Data sets used by a program list.

   Other Reports

7. Control Report DCBBR462, *PROCLIB Members Not Used*

8. Control Report DCBBR482, *PROCLIB Members Not Found*

10.14.1.4 Manual Input

A preprinted form must be completed by the author for new Application code titles and report information.

Application Author Form

1. *JCL Narrative Request. 17805.000* (Figure A). Each monthly process cycle will produce a pre-printed request form for Application/Process codes that require description. The Data Base Administrator (DBA) will forward the request form to the appropriate department in accor-

Through the courtesy of Del Monte Corp.

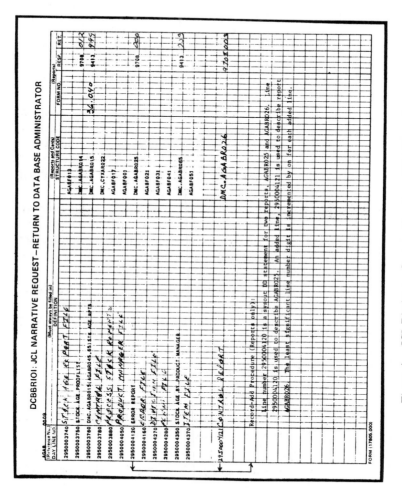

Figure A. JCL Dictionary System. (Courtesy of Del Monte Corp.)

135

dance with the Application/Process code heading the form. Upon completion, the Application author will return the form to the DBA for submission to the next process cycle.

The turnaround request will only transact against the master file that produced it, since the Julian run date is part of the reference line number. Unmatched request transactions are listed, and the next process cycle will list new line numbers for current and unsatisfied prior requests.

A line is printed for each master file record requiring all, or some, request columns to be completed. Data already on the master file is pre-printed in the appropriate columns, so that only blank columns must be completed (left justified always and leading zeros in Retention column).

An Application code title must be provided for every request line. This code is shown in its JCL context by the Job Control Language Narrative Report, DCBBR103 (Figure B). In addition, the following information must also be specified:

a.   Reports and cards. Specify fully qualified (e.g., DMC.XXXXXXXX) structure code, since it is not specified by Job Control Language. When several reports are produced from a single Data Definition Statement (as in MARK IV), add a manual record for each report as specified in Figure A.

Some card data sets (a date card, for instance) do not have a name. For these sets, specify their step name and the literal CARD in the Structure Code Column (e.g., XXXXC010(CARD)).

b.   Reports. Specify responsibility code, retention period in months, and special form (if any). (See Figures C, D, and E).

10.14.1.5 Special Handling of Procedures

To reduce input, resolution of procedure symbolics can be suppressed to permit a one time generic definition, instead of redefining the resolved symbolics each time they are used by a different

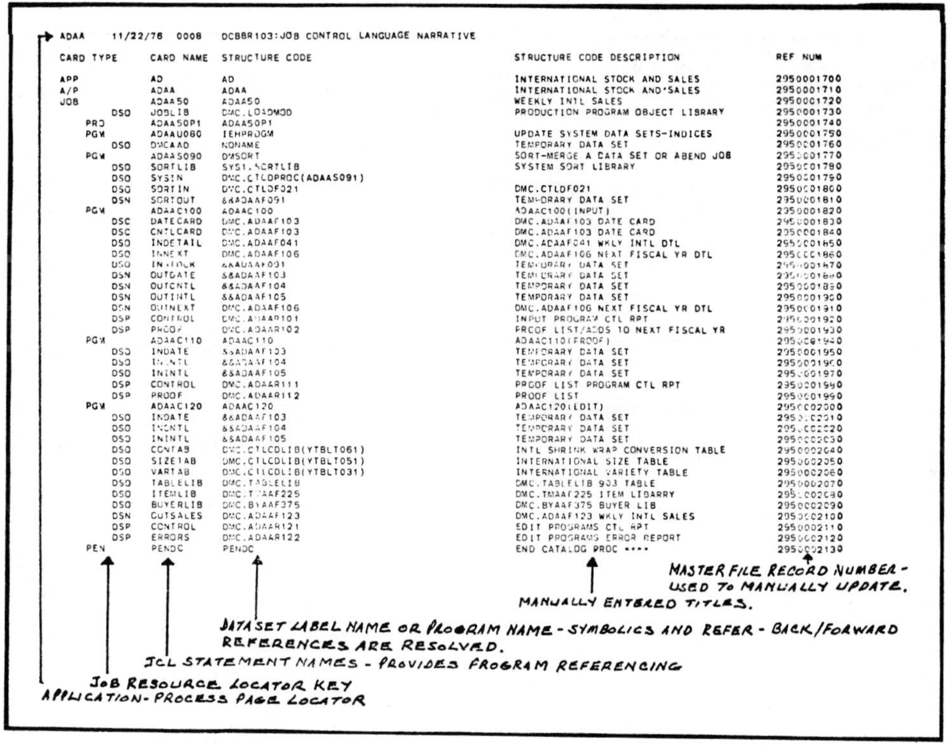

Figure B. JCL Dictionary System. (Courtesy of Del Monte Corp.)

ADAA   11/22/78   0008   DC8BR103:JOB CONTROL LANGUAGE NARRATIVE

CARD TYPE	CARD NAME	STRUCTURE CODE	STRUCTURE CODE DESCRIPTION	REF NUM
APP	ADAA	AD	INTERNATIONAL STOCK AND SALES	2950001700
A/P	ADAA	ADAA	INTERNATIONAL STOCK AND'SALES	2950001710
JOB	ADAA50	ADAA50	WEEKLY INTL SALES	2950001720
PRC	JDBLIB	DMC.LOADMOD	PRODUCTION PROGRAM OBJECT LIBRARY	2950001730
DSD	ADAASOP1	ADAASOP1		2950001740
DSD	ADAAU080	IEHPROGM		2950001750
PGM	DVCAAO	NONAME	UPDATE SYSTEM DATA SETS-INDICES	2950001760
DSD	ADAAS090	DVSORT	TEMPORARY DATA SET	2950001770
DSD	SORTLIB	SYS1.SORTLIB	SORT-MERGE A DATA SET OR ABEND JOB	2950001780
DSN	SYSIN	DMC.CLCOPPROC(ADAAS091)	SYSTEM SORT LIBRARY	2950001790
DSN	SORTIN	DYC.CTLDF021		2950001800
DSN	SORTOUT	&&ADAAKF091	DMC.CTLDF021	2950001810
PGM	ADAAC100	ADAAC100	TEMPORARY DATA SET	2950001820
DSC	DATCARD	DMC.ADAAF103	ADAAC100(INPUT)	2950001830
DSC	CNTLCARD	DMC.ADAAF103	DMC.ADAAF103 DATE CARD	2950001840
DSC	INDETAIL	DMC.ADAAF041	DMC.ADAAF041 WKLY INTL DTL	2950001850
DSD	INNEXT	DMC.ADAAF106	DMC.ADAAF106 NEXT FISCAL YR DTL	2950001860
DSN	INTOTAL	&&ADAAF091	TEMPORARY DATA SET	2950001870
DSN	OUTDATE	&&ADAAF103	TEMPORARY DATA SET	2950001880
DSN	OUTNTL	&&ADAAF104	TEMPORARY DATA SET	2950001890
DSN	OUTINTL	&&ADAAF105	DMC.ADAAF106 NEXT FISCAL YR DTL	2950001900
DSN	OUTNXT	DMC.ADAAF106	TEMPORARY DATA SET	2950001910
DSP	OUTNTL	DMC.ADAAF041	PROOF LIST/ADDS TO NEXT FISCAL YR	2950001920
DSP	PKCFOL	DMC.ADAAF02	ADAAC110(PROOF)	2950001930
PGM	ADAAC110	ADAAC110	TEMPORARY DATA SET	2950001940
DSD	INDATE	&&ADAAF103	TEMPORARY DATA SET	2950001950
DSD	INNTL	&&ADAAF104	TEMPORARY DATA SET	2950001960
DSD	ININTL	&&ADAAF105	TEMPORARY DATA SET	2950001970
DSP	CONTROL	DMC.ADAAR111	PROOF LIST PROGRAM CTL RPT	2950001980
DSP	PROOF	DMC.ADAAR112	PROOF LIST	2950001990
PGM	ADAAC120	ADAAC120	ADAAC120(EDIT)	2950002000
DSD	INDATE	&&ADAAF103	TEMPORARY DATA SET	2950002010
DSD	INCNTL	&&ADAAF104	TEMPORARY DATA SET	2950002020
DSD	ININTL	&&ADAAF105	INTL SHRINK WRAP CONVERSION TABLE	2950002030
DSD	CONTAB	DYC.CTLDLIB(IYTBL1050)	INTERNATIONAL SIZE TABLE	2950002040
DSD	VARTAB	DMC.CTLDLIB(IYTBL1051)	INTERNATIONAL VARIETY TABLE	2950002050
DSD	TABLELIB	DMC.CTLDLIB(IYTBL1031)	DMC.TABLELIB 903 TABLE	2950002060
DSD	ITEMLIB	DMC.T03ELIB	DMC.T0AAF225 ITEM LIBRARY	2950002070
DSD	BUYERLIB	DMC.T0AAF225	DMC.BYAAF375 BUYER LIB	2950002080
DSD	INSALES	DMC.BYAAF375	DMC.BYAAF123 WKLY INTL SALES	2950002090
DSP	CONTROL	DMC.ADAAF121	EDIT PROGRAMS CTL RPT	2950002100
DSP	ERRORS	DMC.ADAAF122	EDIT PROGRAMS ERROR REPORT	2950002120
PEN	PENOC	PENOC	END CATALOG PROC ****	2950002130

(handwritten annotations)
MASTER FILE RECORD NUMBER - USED TO MANUALLY UPDATE.

MANUALLY ENTERED TITLES.

DATASET LABEL NAME OR PROGRAM NAME - SYMBOLICS AND REFER - BACK/FORWARD REFERENCES ARE RESOLVED.

JCL STATEMENT NAMES - PROVIDES PROGRAM REFERENCING.

JOB RESOURCE LOCATOR KEY

APPLICATION - PROCESS PAGE LOCATOR

137

10/22/76 0007	DCBBR121 REPORT DATA SET LISTING SEQUENCED BY RESP CODE				
RPT NUM	REPORT TITLE	FORM NUM	RESP CODE	CUSTODIAN	RET
DMC.PRLDR031	QUARTERLY REPORT	W-2	0375	CALIFORNIA DIVISION	000
DMC.PRLGR011	W-2 FORMS(SPEC U.S. TREASICAL DIV		0375	CALIFORNIA DIVISION	048
DMC.PRPCR011	DAILY EARNINGS REPORT(ALL PLTS)		0375	CALIFORNIA DIVISION	012
DMC.RADAR051	COMMODITY INFORMATION SHEETS	1006-000	0375	CALIFORNIA DIVISION	024
DMC.NPLGR011	EMPLOYEE INFORMATION	1076.0	1375	NORTHWEST DIVISION	
DMC.PVAAR224	SFO CREDIT UNION DEDUCT.RPT		1770	DEL MONTE S.F. FED. CREDIT UNION	036
DMC.CVAWR011	MIDWEST ANNUAL PACK REPORT		3375	MIDWEST DIVISION	036
DVC.TRAYR031	MW ANNUAL INTRA-DIV TRANS SHIPMT PKG		3375	MIDWEST DIVISION	036
DVC.TRAYR041	MW ANNUAL INTER-DIV TRANS RCPTS PKG P		3375	MIDWEST DIVISION	036
DVC.TRAYR051	MW ANNUAL INTRA-DIV TRANS RCPTS PKG P		3375	MIDWEST DIVISION	036
DVC.TRAYR061	MW ANNUAL INTER-DIV TRANS SHIPMT DIST		3375	MIDWEST DIVISION	036
DVC.TRAYR071	MW ANNUAL INTRA-DIV TRANS SHIPMT DIST		3375	MIDWEST DIVISION	036
DVC.TRAYR081	MW ANNUAL INTER-DIV TRANS RCPTS DIST		3375	MIDWEST DIVISION	036
DVC.TRAYR091	MW ANNUAL INTRA-DIV TRANS RCPTS DIST		3375	MIDWEST DIVISION	036
DMC.ADMAR091	M & S MSTR ERROR PROOF LIST		5800	ALASKA PACKERS ASSOCIATION, INC.	000
DMC.AEDAR092	M & S PHYSICAL INV SVC ERROR PROOF		5800	ALASKA PACKERS ASSOCIATION, INC.	000
DMC.AGMA2033	APA M&S MSTR DELETED STOCK NUM.		5800	ALASKA PACKERS ASSOCIATION, INC.	000
DMC.AGMAR096	APA M&S MSTR FILE SVC ERROR RPT		5800	ALASKA PACKERS ASSOCIATION, INC.	000
DMC.AGMAR096	APA MSIM FILL SVCE CONTROL RPT		5900	ALASKA PACKERS ASSOCIATION, INC.	000
DMC.ABLCR071	CONTROL REPORT		5900	ALASKA PACKERS ASSOCIATION, INC.	004
DMC.DVACR032	RECAP OF SALES BROKER/BUYER		8801	U.S. SALES ADMINISTRATION	002
DVC.CVACR032	WEEKLY WAREHOUSED GOODS CONTROL REPOR		8801	U.S. SALES ADMINISTRATION	012
DVC.CTLVR041	STOCK CONTROL TABLES PROOFLIST		9002	PRODUCT MANAGEMENT	060
DMC.O.ACR035	RECAP OF TOTAL MILITARY SALES BY REGI		9002	PRODUCT MANAGEMENT	060
DMC.O.ALR036	RECAP OF SALES TO MILITARY ACCTS BY D		9002	PRODUCT MANAGEMENT	060
DMC.OPLAR102	GOVT.PRICING PROOF/ERROR LIST		9002	PRODUCT MANAGEMENT	036
DMC.OPACR031	PRODUCT BROKERAGE REPORT (MONTHLY)		9005	INT'L MARKETING SERVICES	024
DMC.DE.GR041	DMI BROKERAGE REPORT		9005	INT'L MARKETING SERVICES	
DMC.EWAAR022	DMI QUARTERLY BILLINGS(AREA II)		9005	INT'L MARKETING SERVICES	012
DMC.EWAAR062	CONTROL REPORT 1		9005	INT'L MARKETING SERVICES	012
DMC.EWAAR063	TARGET CHANGES BY COUNTRY		9005	INT'L MARKETING SERVICES	012
DMC.EWA9R164	CONTROL REPORT 1		9005	INT'L MARKETING SERVICES	024
DMC.EWA9R165	INTL SALES FIVE YEAR PACK/SALE		9005	INT'L MARKETING SERVICES	024
DMC.EWA9R271	ERROR RPT NON-MATCH ITEMS		9005	INT'L MARKETING SERVICES	024
DMC.EWA9R332	LIST OF INTL SALES ESTIMTBLE		9005	INT'L MARKETING SERVICES	024
DVC.EWA9R333	INTL SALES TOTAL RECAP BY PLT		9005	INT'L MARKETING SERVICES	024
DVC.EWA9R334	INTL SALES TOTAL VAR RECAP BY MKT		9005	INT'L MARKETING SERVICES	024
DMC.EWA9R335	INTL SALES TOTAL VAR RECAP BY MAJ REG		9005	INT'L MARKETING SERVICES	024
DMC.EWA9R336	INTL SALES VARIETY TOTAL RECAP		9005	INT'L MARKETING SERVICES	024
DMC.EWA9R337	INTL SALES ERROR LIST-MKT/PLT/VAR		9005	INT'L MARKETING SERVICES	024
DMC.CYAAR061	TOTAL VARIETY RECAP BY MARKET AND PLA	11626.13	9005	INT'L MARKETING SERVICES	024
DMC.CYAOR021	DW RECORD OF O.D INTL		9005	INT'L MARKETING SERVICES	024
DMC.CYAOR022	INTL.GOALS UPDATE ERROR LIST		9005	INT'L MARKETING SERVICES	024
DMC.CYAOR025	INTL.GOALS.VAR.SIZE ERROR LIST		9005	INT'L MARKETING SERVICES	024
DMC.CYAOR071	INTL MARKETING CONTROL RPT #1		9005	INT'L MARKETING SERVICES	024
DMC.CYADR091	ERROR LISTING		9005	INT'L MARKETING SERVICES	024
DMC.CYADR093	CONTROL REPORT 2		9005	INT'L MARKETING SERVICES	024
DVC.CYADR094	TARGET DATA BY COUNTRY		9005	INT'L MARKETING SERVICES	024
DMC.CYADR101	CONTROL REPORT 3		9005	INT'L MARKETING SERVICES	999

ONLY SPECIAL PRE-PRINTED FORMS ARE LISTED. XEROX OVER-LAYS ARE NOT LISTED. JCL FORM SUB-PARAMETER IS INITIALLY LISTED, IF USED. IT CAN BE MANUALLY CHANGED OR DELETED, IF DESIRED.

RETENTION - MONTHS

Figure C. JCL Dictionary System. (Courtesy of Del Monte Corp.)

```
06/15/76   DCBBR462:  PROCLIB MEMBERS NOT USED
AMAE10P1
ARBA30P1
ARBA40P1
ARBA50P1
ARBA50P2
BYAA35                        PROCLIB PURGE CANDIDATES
CAPE10P1
CBAJ30P1
CBAK20P1
CEAA30P1
CEAC15P1
CEAD25P1
CEAM17P1
CEBF10P1
CECB20P1
CGAA25P1
CGAA30P1
CGAA30P2
CGAA30P3
CGAA35P1
CGAC25
CGAC30
CGAC35
CGAC40
CGAC50
CGAD25P1
CGAD30P1
CGAD35
CGAD35P1
CGAD40P1
CGAD50P1
CGAD50P2
CGBA20
CGBA20P1
CGBA60
CGCA20
CGDA30
CGDC80
CGDC96
CGDC96P1
CMAB20P1
CMAC20P1
CMAC30P1
CMAC40P1
CMAC50P1
CMAC60P1
CMAC70P1
CMAD20P1
CMAD40P1
CMAF30P1
CMAF30P2
CMAR05P1
CMAR10P1
CMAR15P1
CMAT05P1
CMAT10P1
CMAT15P1
CMAT20P1
CNBB40P1
```

Figure D.   JCL Dictionary System. (Courtesy of Del Monte Corp.)

```
06/10/76  DCBBR482: PROCLIB MEMBERS NOT FOUND
EMJCL11
EMJCL13
S70743
S70743
EMJCL11
SORTD
SORTD
SORTD
SORTD
SORTD
SORTD
SORTD
SORTD
SORTD
SORTD
SORTD
SORTD
EMJCL13
S70743
EM7074
S70743
EMJCL11
S70743
S70743
SORTT
SORTD
DMCWRIT
SORTD
SORTD
SORTD
EMJCL05
EMJCL04
EMJCL01
SORT
UPDTE
SORT
EMJCL11
S70743
EM7074
S70743
S70743
SORTT
SORTT
SORTT
SORTT
SORTT
SORTT
SORTT
SORTT
SORTT
SORTT
SORTD
SORTD
SORTD
SORTD
XSORTD
SORTD
EMJCL11
EMJCL13
```

PROCLIB ADD CANDIDATES

Figure E. JCL Dictonary System. (Courtesy Del Monte Corp.)

job. To suppress, the procedure must contain a PROC Statement named NORESOLV.

Remote Job Entry procedures, not normally on the JCL backup file used by this sytem, can be added to a dummy job set up on the file for this purpose named REMOTER.

10.14.2 DATA DICTIONARY SYSTEM

10.14.2.1 Descriptive Overview

The JCL Dictionary described in the preceding Section (10.14.1) identifies, describes, and cross references Application codes used by Job Control Language (JCL) from Applications down through data sets.

The *Data* Dictionary System extends that system to identify, describe, and cross reference data sets, Copy and TOTAL DBGEN Library members used by the data sets, Copy and TOTAL DBGEN Library elements, and glossary definitions assigned to the Copy and DBGEN elements.

Application authors, in response to a computer-generated turnaround form, link the JCL non-temporary data sets of the JCL Dictionary with Copy and TOTAL DBGEN Library members used by the sets. Authors also assign a glossary number to each Copy and TOTAL DBGEN Library element to link it with its glossary name and definition. (Both linkages may be intentionally bypassed if desired.)

The linkages are used to cross reference:

a.   Data sets with their Copy and DBGEN Library members.

b.   Copy and DBGEN Library elements with their glossary names-definitions.

c.   Glossary names-definitions with data sets and their Copy and DBGEN Library member names.

10.14.2.2 Dictionary Report Output

The existing Copy Library microfiche file containing the new Copy element glossary numbers, and new reference and cross reference books (Books 4 and 5) are filed at the Remotes service counter along with the reference books (Books 1, 2, and 3) of the JCL Dictionary System. All of these books (1 through 5) and the Copy microfiche are used separately, or in combination, to research an Application and to assess the impact of changing an Application.

TOTAL Data Base DBGENs, on DMT.PANLIB, containing the new element glossary numbers are available for listing, using TSO PANVALET commands (Time Sharing Services 5.400).

COPY LIBRARY and TOTAL DBGEN Listings

EXHIBIT

1. Microfiche. DMC.COPYLIB, *Copy Library Listing*
   Each Copy Library Member Name is listed. The elements of all COPYLIB members used by non-temporary data sets are assigned glossary numbers. Number lookup on the Glossary Definitions by Number Listing provides an element definition.

2. TSO Listing. DMT.PANLIB, *TOTAL DBGEN Listing*
   Each TOTAL DBGEN Member with a glossary number assigned to each element is available for listing.

REFERENCE BOOKS

3. Book 4.   DCBBR282, *Glossary Definitions by Number Listing*
   A list of glossary numbers with their glossary names and definitions provides definitions in number sequence.

4. Book 5.   DCBBR283, *Glossary Number-Name Reference Listing*
   A list of glossary names with their glossary numbers provides a number-name cross reference.

5. DCBBR332, *Data Set Cross Reference Listing*
   A list of Copy Library and TOTAL DBGEN Members used by a data set. An asterisk in place of a Copy or DBGEN Member Name specifies no member for the data set. An asterisk after the member name specifies no glossary numbers for its elements.

6. DCBBR235, *COPYLIB and DBGEN Member Cross Reference Listing.*
   A list of data sets defined by a Copy or DBGEN Library member.

7. DCBBR281, *Glossary Number Cross Reference Listing*
   A list of data sets and their Copy Library member names using a glossary number.

Through the courtesy of Del Monte Corp.

8. PVCPR161, *COPY Statement Cross Reference report*
   A list of DMC.COPYLIB members showing the DMC.PANLIB members referencing them.

10.14.2.3 Manual Input

A. DCBBR232, *Copy Library Member Name Request Form (Figure A)*

Departments responsible for maintaining non-temporary data sets must specify the Copy and TOTAL DBGEN Library member names used by these sets, in response to a preprinted turnaround form issued by this system.

For sets that do not use a member or to intentionally omit a member, specify an asterisk as the member name.

To omit glossary numbers intentionally for the Copy or DBGEN elements, specify an asterisk in the Bypass column that immediately follows the record name.

B. DCBBR251, *Glossary Number Request List (Figure B).*

A glossary number is specified on each element record of the Document Utility when a member is initially added to the Copy Library (10.5.5). The Utility, in turn, generates a glossary number comment record (Figure C) for each element. This system produces a Glossary Number Request for missing glossary numbers. In response to the form, numbers are added to existing Copy Library elements by adding glossary number comment records using the IEBUPDTE utility (10.3.12).

For TOTAL DBGENs on DMT.PANLIB, a glossary number is specified in columns 68–72 of each DBGEN data element record when the DBGEN is initially added to the library, or in response to the Glossary Number Request Form issued by this system (Figure D).

If a copy or DBGEN element cannot be assigned an existing glossary number, Data Base Administration will provide a new number, name, and definition to be used.

143

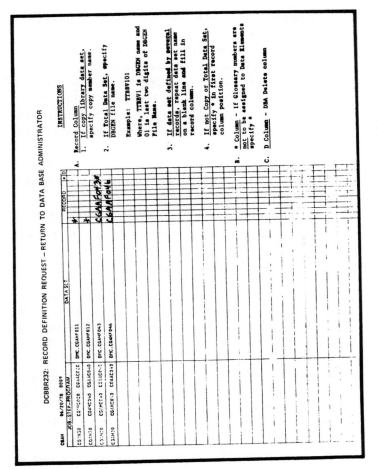

Figure A. Data Dictionary System. (Courtesy of Del Monte Corp.)

0012 RRCF   06/20/78   DCBBR251: COPYLIB GLOSSARY NUMBER REQUEST

MEMBER	SEQ NUM		RECORD ELEMENT			
RRCFD522	000480	15	PROMOTION-IND-SF	PIC X(4).		
RRCFD522	000490	10	REPLEN-PLANT-IND-SF	PIC X.		
RRCFD522	000500	10	RESTR-INDIC-SF	PIC X.		
RRCFD522	000690	10	SHIP-TO-DATE-1-SF	PIC S9(7)	COMP-3.	
RRCFD522	000700	10	SHIP-THIS-WK-1-SF	PIC S9(7)	COMP-3.	
RRCFD522	000710	10	4-WK-SHIP-SF	PIC S9(7)	COMP-3.	
RRCFD522	000780	10	SHIP-TO-DATE-2-SF	PIC S9(7)	COMP-3.	
RRCFD522	000790	10	SHIP-THIS-WK-2-SF	PIC S9(7)	COMP-3.	
RRCFD522	000860	05	SC-NET-AVAILABLE-SF	PIC S9(7)	COMP-3.	
RRCFD522	000900	05	STOCK-CONTROL-INDICATORS-SF.			
RRCFD522	000930	10	NORMALLY-STOCKED-IND-SF	PIC X.		001
RRCFD522	000940	10	CASES-ON-HOLD-IND-SF	PIC X.		001
RRCFD522	001660	10	SM-ACTIVITY-COUNT-SF	PIC S9(7)	COMP-3.	00400197
RRCFD522	001710	15	SM-CASES-IN-PROCESS	PIC S9(7)	COMP-3.	00400201
RRCFD522	001750	15	SM-CS-PEND-SF	PIC S9(7)	COMP-3.	00400205
RRCFD522	001790	15	SM-CS-NET-AVAIL-SF	PIC S9(7)	COMP-3.	00400209
RRCFD522	001930	15	OP-PHASES-SF	PIC X.		00100213
RRCFD522	002000	10	OP-ACTIVITY-COUNT-SF	PIC S9(7)	COMP-3.	00400217
RRCFD522	002080	15	OP-CS-PEND-SF	PIC S9(7)	COMP-3.	00400225
RRCFD522	002120	15	OP-CS-NET-AVAIL-SF	PIC S9(7)	COMP-3.	00400229
RRCFD522	002170	10	PATH-INDIC-SF	PIC X.		
RRCFD522	002180	10	LEVEL-INDIC-SF	PIC X.		
RRCFD522	002190	10	EOP-INDIC-SF	PIC X.		
RRCFD522	002200	10	BRAND-CODE-INDIC-SF	PIC X.		
RRCFD522	002210	10	PINE-INDIC-SF	PIC X.		
RRCFD522	002220	10	ORD-OUT-INDIC-SF	PIC X.		
RRCFT171	000390	10	PT-PD-FROM-ZONE	PIC X.		00100054
RRCFT171	000400	10	PT-SALVAGE-PERCENT	PIC XX.		00200056
RRCFT171	000700	10	ST-TERM-ID	PIC XX.		00200028
RRCFT171	000710	10	ST-TERM-CNTRL	PIC X.		00100029

INSTRUCTIONS:
1. COPYLIB. Add glossary number comment record after each data record (Seqnum in 1-6, * in 7 & 75, Glossary number in 76-80).
2. TOTAL DBGEN. Add glossary number in 68-72 of Data and Control records (exclude Link records).

Figure B. Data Dictionary System

Copy Library Member Listing, Incorporating
Data Dictionary Glossary Number Comment Records

```
 JJJJ13 01  SA-DETAL.                                              AMAAFJ51
 JJJ02C*                                                            *J2JJ4
 JJJJJJ       05  REC-CODE-SA  PIC X.
 JJJJ43*                                                           *J2JU5
 UJJJ5C       05  COMP-CODE-SA PIC X.
 JJJJ6J*                                                           *15JJ1
 JJJJ75       J5  PROCESS-DT-SA.
 UUJ28J*                                                           *J85J1
 UJJJ9J           1J  PROCESS-YR-SA   PIC 99.
 JJJ1JJ*                                                           *J95C1
 JJJ11J           1J  PROCESS-MO-SA   PIC 99.
 JJJ12J*                                                           *J85J1
 JUJ13J           1J  PROCESS-DA-SA   PIC 99.
 JJJ14J*                                                           *J85J1
 JJJ15J       J5  SEJ-CODE-SA PIC XXX.                            00300J11
 UJJ16C*                                                           *J74J1
 JJJ17J       05  SHP-DIV-SA  PIC XX.                             JJ2JJJ13
 J-J18J*                                                           *02JJ4
 JJJ19J       05  CASES-SA    PIC S9(7) CCMP-3.
 JJJ2JJ*                                                           *14JJ3
 JUJ21C
 JJJ22J       05  AMOUNT-SA                PICTURE S9(7)V99 COMP-3.
 JJJ23J*                                                           *JJ4J4
 JUJ24J
 JJJ25J       05  ACCOUNT-SA PIC X(4).                            JJ4JJJ26
 JJJ26J*                                                           *J2J1
 JUJ27J       05  RESP-CO-SA PIC X(4).                            JJ4JJJ3J
 JJJ28J*                                                           *J75JJ
 JJJ29J       J5  SUB-CO-SA  PIC X(4).                            JJ4JJJ34
 JJJ3JJ*                                                           *J3132
 JJJ31J       05  SEC-SUB-SA PIC X(6).                            JJ6JJJ45
 JJJ32J*                                                           *JJ1J3
 JJJ33J       05  COMMODITY-SA PIC X(3).                          JJ3JJJ43
 JJJ34J*                                                           *J3132
 JUJ35J       05  INV-KD-SA  PIC XX.                              JJ2JJJ45
 JJJ36J*                                                           *J37J1
 JJJ37J       J5  SECT-CO-SA PIC XX.                              JJ2JJJ47
 JJJ38J*                                                           *12531
 JJJ39J       05  PROD-CO-SA PIC XX.                              JJ2JJJ49
 JJJ4JJ*                                                           *12801
 JUJ41C       05  DMSC-SALE-SA          PIC 9.
 JJJ42J*                                                           *15JJ1
 JJJ43J       05  PLANT-SA              PIC XXX.
 JJJ44J*                                                           *12JJ1
 JJJ45J       05  FILLER      PIC X.
 UJJ46C*                                                           *J2JJ1
 JJJ47J       05  SALES-ANAL-CO-SA PIC XX.                        JJ2JJJ5J
 JJJ48J*                                                           *J2JJ5
```

→ A glossary number is specified for each Copy Library element by a
Glossary Number Comment Record. The record must contain a sequence
number (cols 1-6) to properly position the record after the element
record, asterisks (cols 7 and 75), and a five digit glossary number
(cols 76-80).

Figure C. Data Dictionary System (Courtesy of Del Monte Corp.)

146

```
08/17/77   0037  DCBBR292: GLOSSARY DEFINITIONS BY NUMBER LISTING

12801     PRODUCT CODE

    001        1. A NUMBER CODE ASSIGNED TO A VARIETY CODE TO GROUP
    005           VARIETY CODES INTO THE MORE GENERALIZED PRODUCT
    010           CLASSIFICATIONS.
    020           EXAMPLE: 01= FRUITS, JUICES, NECTARS
    025                    07= CITRUS
    035                    10= PINEAPPLE

12802     PRODUCT CODE - INTERNATIONAL

    001        1. A NUMBER CODE ASSIGNED TO AN INTERNATIONAL VARIETY
    005           CODE TO GROUP INTERNATIONAL VARIETY CODES INTO A
    010           MORE GENERALIZED PRODUCT CLASSIFICATION.
    015           EXAMPLE: 10 = FRUITS
    020                    20 = NECTARS AND DRINKS
    025                    40 = PINEAPPLE PRODUCTS

12803     PRODUCT CODE - BROKERAGE

    001        1. A NUMBER CODE ASSIGNED TO A PRODUCT CODE SPECIFYING
    005           ONE OF THE SIX PRODUCT CATEGORIES ELIGIBLE FOR
    010           BROKERAGE PAYMENT.
    015           EXAMPLE: 01 = CANNED FOOD
    020                    02 = CITRUS
    025                    03 = APRICOTS PITS
    030                    04 = DRIED FRUIT (DEL MONTE)
    035                    05 = FISH
    040                    06 = DRIED FRUIT (OTHER BRANDS)
    050        2. REFER AMOUNT-BROKERAGE

12901     STRUCTURE NUMBER

    001        1. AN 8 DIGIT NUMBER ASSIGNED TO ALLOWANCE AND GENERAL POSTING
    005           PRICE RECORDS TO GROUP RECORDS FOR UPDATING IN THE INVOICE
    010           PRICING SYSTEM.
    015        2. THIS CODE IDENTIFIES THE STRUCTURE TYPE, PRODUCT GROUP TYPE
    020           AND POSTING NUMBER.
    025              XX = STRUCTURE TYPE REFER 27150
    030              XX = PRODUCT GROUP CODE-PRICING REFER 27290
    035              XXXX = SEQUENTIAL NUMBER

13001     WEIGHT SPREAD CODE

    001        1. A NUMBER CODE ASSIGNED TO A VARIETY CODE SPECIFYING
    005           AN INTER-STATE COMMERCE COMMISSION PRODUCT CATEGORY.
    010           EXAMPLE: 1 = CANNED FOOD
    015                    2 = PINEAPPLE
    020                    3 = DRIED FRUIT
    025                    9 = OUTSIDE ENCLOSURES
```

Figure D.   Data Dictionary System (Courtesy of Del Monte Corp.)

11

OVERVIEW
OF COMMERCIAL DATA
DICTIONARY / DIRECTORY
SYSTEM PACKAGES

To complete the information on automated data dictionaries, the commercially available data dictionary/directory (DD/D) systems are discussed in this chapter.

Whether the commercial package is a "stand-alone" DD/D, i.e., it functions separately from the data base(s) or the DBMS; a "dependent" DD/D, i.e., it is tailored to a specific system and used as front end to the particular data base(s) or DBMS; or a DD/D "merged" into the DBMS, i.e., it is fully integrated with the DBMS, it can enhance the data control and management capabilities of the particular system.

Insofar as access methods are concerned, the DD/D may use ISAM, VSAM, BDAM, or the installed DBMS file structure (the latter for direct accessing). Naturally, the DBMS vendors who also market data dictionaries use the direct accessing method with their own system.

11.1 STAND-ALONE VERSUS DEPENDENT DDD SOFTWARE

Perhaps at this point benefits of the stand-alone and the dependent DD/D packages should be mentioned.

11.1.1 The principal advantages of stand-alone DD/D software packages are the following:

a. They are self-contained and perform their basic functions of identifying, defining, storing, controlling, and managing information about data elements and data items independently of any data base(s) or DBMS.

b. They have the ability to store information about computer data as well as nonmechanized data.

c. They can support one or more DBMS (sometimes simultaneously) through their interfacing capability. (This feature increases the effectiveness of both the DBMS and the dictionary.)

11.1.2 The principal advantages of dependent (and more specifically of merged) DD/D software packages are the following:

a. They provide information as to the location of data within the physical data bases.

b. They provide data validation through embedded range and criteria checking. (This feature enhances the integrity of both data and the DD/D.)

c. They provide a record of data access and terminal access against sensitive data elements, records, and files.

11.2 DATA DICTIONARY SELECTION CRITERIA

In selecting a commercially available dictionary package, some or all of the following criteria should be considered, depending on the individual environment.

1. Is it a dependent or a stand-alone DD/D?
2. Does it have both batch and online capabilities?
3. Is its chief function to control and manage data elements and their relationships?
4. Does it provide up-to-date documentation?
5. Does it provide more than standard security features against possible computer abuse and fraud?
6. Does it provide an automatic interface to existing programs?
7. Does it have the ability to generate custom-tailored reports?
8. Does it produce audit-trail reports?
9. Does it provide COPYing facilities?
10. Is it flexible enough to allow structural change of data elements?
11. Does it have the capability to produce reports that show the effect that structural change of data element(s) has on the DD/D system?
12. What kind of file update capability does it provide?
13. What are its file backup provisions and its recovery capabilities?
14. Is it simple enough so that nontechnical personnel can use it also?

The following paragraphs provide a more detailed discussion of these criteria:

1. Is It a Dependent or a Stand-Alone DD/D? A DD/D designed for and based on a specific DBMS and (as currently advocated) merged into it may provide greater advantages and more capabilities in a particular environment. However, it must be pointed out that when a DD/D is merged with a DBMS, it could result in an increase of the software overhead cost. This

151

may occur because its logic could affect the DBMS' performance. An example of such occurrence would be having the application programs move through the DD/D's verification routines, whether it is necessary or not. On the other hand, depending on the particular environment, a stand-alone DD/D that can automatically interface to one or more DBMS and can generate data elements independently of the operating DBMS may be more useful and cost significantly less.

2. Does It Have both Batch and Online Capabilities? While most commercially available dictionary packages are designed to run in both batch and online interactive environments, it is still a good idea to check that the product in addition to batch processing supports online updating and keyword search query.

3. Is Its Chief Function to Control and Manage Data Elements and Their Relationships? Regardless whether the DD/D is stand-alone or part of a DBMS, it should be more than just a reservoir of information about data elements, a catalog of system definitions, and a cross-referencing and report generating tool. Its main functions should be identifying, defining, describing, storing, locating, and controlling data elements and their relationships, as well as managing information about them.

4. Does it Provide Up-to-Date Documentation? The DD/D should provide uniform, current documentation to enforce standards and reduce inconsistency and redundancy of definitions and descriptions. In addition, documentation that conveys where each data element, record, and data set is used facilitates assessing the impact of a proposed change on the system.

5. Does It Provide More than Standard Security Features Against Possible Computer Abuse and Fraud? Since all the information about the corporate data is stored in the dictionary data base, it is imperative that effective security features are an integral part of the package. Periodic change of passwords and restrictive access to unique data elements, records, and files are not sufficient security measures anymore in this age of sophisticated computer crimes. For example, it would be comparatively easy for a skilled programmer/analyst to analyze corporate data through the relationships described in the DD/D and to use that data to perpetrate a fraud. Consequently, it is highly desirable that the commercial product, just as the inhouse developed data dictionary, have—at minimum—the additional capability of retaining access path logic for recurring update requests.

6. Does It Provide an Automatic Interface to Existing Programs? Since established DP facilities run many application programs in COBOL, BASIC, PL/1, ALC, etc., it is very important that the dictionary has the capability to create automatically data entries from the data divisions of the already existing programs.

7. Does It Have the Ability to Generate Custom-Tailored Reports? Whereas all available commercial dictionaries provide a great number of standardized reports, the DD/D should also have the ability to generate ad hoc, free-form reports. In addition, for truly user-tailored reports, it should provide a USER EXIT capability to allow customized editing of input.

8. Does It Produce Audit-Trail Reports? Both company and outside auditors are concerned with the control and accuracy of information and the efficient processing of data. Consequently, the DD/D should provide audit-trail reports, so that the auditors can audit and evaluate the system for effectiveness, reliability, and timeliness.

9. Does It Provide COPYing Facilities? If the package is to be a significant aid to the programming staff, it should provide the capability of automatically generating data descriptions as well as higher language codes from definitions stored in the DD/D.

10. Is It Flexible Enough to Allow Structural Change of Data Elements? Since in certain circumstances it is necessary for the systems analyst/designer to change the structure of a particular data element(s), it is desirable for the package to have the ability to accommodate specific changes of data types through "change control" mode.

11. Does It Have the Capability to Generate Reports that Show the Impact that Structural Change in Data Element(s) Has on the System? Since this information is essential to the systems analyst/designer who is making a structural change in data element(s), such reports should be provided by the DD/D to effect a more accurate estimate as to the "follow-up" tasks.

12. What Kind of File Update Capability Does It Provide? Is the file update "single-entry," i.e., does it automatically update each occurrence of the affected entry? Or is it "individual" file update, i.e., does the DD/D update only the specified occurrences, while other occurrences have to be updated individually? The selection depends on requirements, environment, and management policy on "trade-offs."

13. What Are Its File Backup Provisions and Its Recovery Capabilities? For the integrity of the system, it is crucial to have appropriate file backup provisions and recovery capabilities in case of system failure.

14. Is It Simple Enough For Nontechnical Personnel? Last but definitely not least is the criterion of whether the dictionary is easy to use? Since it has become an accepted practice to have not only the data base administrator, systems analysts/designers, and programmers access and utilize information contained in the DD/D but auditors, general management, and certain clerical staff as well, it is quite important that the dictionary cater to the latter group also. Specifically, the DD/D should provide, in addition to COBOL, PL/1, ALC, or other high-level programming languages, an English-like command language, a simple input and online query language in free-form or fixed-form. Tutorials that "guide" as well as "prompt" are also very useful to the non-DP users. These are significant points, because very often the success or failure of a DD/D depends on the non-DP users' acceptance or rejection of the package.

The last criterion, ease of use, seems to become increasingly important to enterprises in selecting a particular data dictionary package. The reason is that in addition to including the non-DP staff among the users of the considered system, many firms don't want the added expense of having high salaried analysts or senior programmers do the physical loading of the data elements.

At more and more facilities clerks are being trained and then assigned to key in descriptions of data elements at terminals. Clerks are also used to fill in previously designed forms to define the entities that will be included in the DD/D.

This not only saves money for the particular firms— the difference between analysts' or senior programmers' salaries and clerks' salaries—but it also frees the DP professionals to load files, records, and programs from the mainframe, thus expediting the implementation of the data dictionary.

The charts on the next five pages present a visual summary of the BASIC features of the better known commercially available DD/D software packages for mainframes and minis. The matrix is followed by a sample of one of the widely used commercially available data dictionaries: UCC TEN DATA DICTIONARY/MANAGER—An Overview.

Name of Software Package	Vendor	Proprietary?	Hardware Required
DATA CATALOGUE 2	Synergetics Corporation	Yes	IBM 360/370 Univac 1100
DATA DICTIONARY	Cincom Systems, Inc.	Yes	IBM 360/370
DB/DC DATA DICTIONARY SYSTEMS	IBM	Yes	IBM 370
DATAMANAGER	MSP Inc.	Yes	IBM 360/370 4300
LEXICON*	Arthur Andersen & Co.	Yes	IBM 360/370 IBM System 3
UCC TEN—THE DATA DICTIONARY/ MANAGER	University Computing Company	Yes	IBM 360/370
DICTIONARY/3000	Imacs Systems Corporation	Yes	HP 3000

*Arthur Anderson & Co. no longer offers LEXICON to new users. Existing users will continue to be supported, and will be assisted in their migration to a dictionary (such as IBM's DB/DC) closely integrated with their DBMS.

Available Data Dictionary/Directory System Packages

Operating System	Operational Mode	Running Environment	Use of DBMS
OS; OS/VS DOS; DOS/VS EXEC-8	Batch and Online	Test and Production	Supports IMS, IMS/DLI, TOTAL, ADABAS, DMS/1100, & MARK IV. Interfaces to S2000 & IDMS
OS/MFT; OS/MVT OS/VS; DOS/VS	Batch	Test and Production	Requires TOTAL
OS/VS; DOS/VS	Batch and Online	Test and Production	Requires IMS/VS or DLI DOS/VS
OS; OS/VS DOS; DOS/VS JOS/VSE	Batch and Online	Test and Production	Interfaces to IMS, IMS/DLI, IDMS, S2000, ADABAS, MARK IV, TOTAL
OS/MFT; OS/MVS VS; DOS/MVT	Batch and Online	Test and Production	Interfaces to IMS, IDMS, TOTAL
OS; OS/VS	Batch and Online	Test and Production	Requires IMS/360/370 or IMS/VS
HP's MPE/OS	Batch and Online	Test and Production	Requires HP's IMAGE

157

Name of Package	Data Structure	Type of Files Supported	Kind of File Update
DATA CATALOGUE 2	Hierarchical	OS, DOS, UNIVAC, IMS, IMS/DLI, TOTAL ADABAS, S2000, IDMS, MARK IV files	Single-entry
DATA DICTIONARY	Network	TOTAL Files	Single-entry for data items; Individual for synonyms
DB/DC DATA DICTIONARY SYSTEMS	Hierarchical	IMS, OS Files	Single-entry and Individual
DATAMANAGER	Hierarchical	IMS, OS Files, IDMS, ADABAS, S2000, TOTAL Files	Single-entry
LEXICON	Hierarchical, Network, and Relational	IMS, OS Files IDMS, TOTAL Files	Single-entry
UCC TEN—THE DATA DICTIONARY/ MANAGER	Hierarchical	IMS, OS Files	Single-entry
DICTIONARY/3000	Hierarchical	IMAGE, KSAM, or Sequential Files	Single-entry and Individual

Available Data Dictionary/Directory System Packages

File Backup and Recovery	Output Form	Automatic Interface to Existing Programs?	Character Type
DATA CATALOGUE Utilities	Hard copy and Microfilm	Yes	Alpha, numeric, alphanumeric, and special
IBM and TOTAL Utilities	Hard copy	Yes	Alpha, numeric, alphanumeric, and special
IMS Utilities	Hard copy	Yes	Alpha, numeric, alphanumeric, and special
DATA- MANAGER Utilities	Hard copy and Microfilm	Yes	Alpha, numeric, alphanumeric, and special
IBM Utilities	Hard copy and Microfilm	Yes	Alpha, numeric, alphanumeric, and special
IMS Utilities	Hard copy	Yes	Alpha, numeric, alphanumeric, and special
HP Utilities	Hard copy	Yes	Alpha, numeric, alphanumeric, and special

Name of Package	Programming Language	Command Language	Input Language
DATA CATALOGUE 2	ANS COBOL	Free-form	Free-form from application programs & from IMS DBDs & PSBs
DATA DICTIONARY	ALC	Free-form	Fixed-form "initial load"; Free-form keyword-oriented
DB/DC DATA DICTIONARY SYSTEMS	ALC	Free-form	Free-form command lang.; Fixed-form "interactive display forms; DBMS data def; From appl. programs
DATAMANAGER	ALC	Free-form	Free-form definition language
LEXICON	ALC and ANS COBOL	Free-form Report Definition Language	Free-form def. language (English-like)
UCC TEN—THE DATA DICTIONARY/ MANAGER	ALC AND ANS COBOL	Free-form transaction driven	Free-form command language; Fixed-form; keyword-oriented; 3270 "menu"
DICTIONARY/3000	MASTER 3000 (own language)	Free-form	Free-form def. language (Eng.-like)

Available Data Dictionary/Directory System Packages

Online Queries?	Online Query Language	Tutorial?	Data Representation
Yes	Free-form; Query through KWIC indexes	Yes through help command	1. Length 2. Type 3. Usage 4. Picture 5. Justification 6. Synchronization
No	N.A.	No	1. Length 2. Type 3. Usage 4. Picture
Yes	Fixed-form through "interactive display forms" facility	Yes, through "interactive display forms" facility	1. Length 2. Type 3. Usage 4. Picture 5. Justification 6. Synchronization
Yes	Free-form	Yes, through an "example dictionary"	1. Length 2. Type 3. Usage 4. Picture 5. Justification 6. Synchronization
Yes	Free-form	Yes	1. Length 2. Type 3. Usage 4. Picture
Yes	Free-form; keyword-oriented through 3270 "menu"	Yes, through 3270 "menu"	1. Length 2. Type 3. Usage 4. Picture 5. Justification
Yes	Free-form through Master 3000 "menu"	Yes	1. Length 2. Type 3. Usage 4. Picture

Name of Software Package	Allows Synonyms?	Validation/ Editing Performed By	Redundancy/Incon- sistency Check?
DATA CATALOGUE 2	Yes	DD/D facility	Yes DD/D facility
DATA DICTIONARY	Yes	DD/D facility	Yes DBMS facility
DB/DC DATA DIC- TIONARY SYSTEMS	Yes	DD/D facility and User- written	Yes DD/D facility
DATAMANAGER	Yes	DD/D facility	Yes DD/D facility
LEXICON	Yes	DD/D facility	Yes DD/D facility
UCC TEN—THE DATA DICTIONARY MANAGER	Yes	DD/D facility and User-written	Yes DD/D facility and "softw. switch"
DICTIONARY/3000	Yes	D/3000 facility and User-written	Yes D/3000 facility

Available Data Dictionary/Directory System Packages

Definition/ Description	Relationships Capability?	Cross Reference Capability?	Error Checking Capability?
Yes Narrative description	Yes	Yes	Yes
Yes Narrative description	Yes	Yes	Yes
Yes Narrative description, and "User data"	Yes	Yes	Yes
Yes Narrative description	Yes	Yes	Yes
Yes Narrative description	Yes	Yes	Yes
Yes Narr. descript. and Summary definition	Yes	Yes	Yes
Yes Narrative description	Yes	Yes	Yes

Name of Software Package	Generation of Copylib and DBMS Control Blocks	Security
DATA CATALOGUE 2	1. DBD 2. PSB 3. Copylib 4. SSA 5. Schemes 6. Subschemas	Three types of passwords; security at element level may be specified
DATA DICTIONARY	1. DBD 2. PSB 3. Copylib 4. SSA	Password facility; security at elem. level may be specified; additional security through "user exit"
DB/DC DATA DICTIONARY SYSTEMS	1. DBD 2. PSB 3. Copylib 4. SSA	IMS and op. system: IMS/VS sec. subsystem; IMS terminal
DATAMANAGER	1. DBD 2. PSB 3. Copylib 4. SSA	Password facility; security assigned at 3 levels (access, alter, remove)
LEXICON	1. DBD 2. PSB 3. Copylib 4. SSA	DD/D special security module; security assigned at 3 levels; user supplied password
UCC TEN—THE DATA DICTIONARY/ MANAGER	1. DBD 2. PSB 3. Copylib 4. SSA 5. SYSGEN 6. PCB 7. MFS 8. RSA 9. GIS DDTs 10. ADF Rules	IMS and operating system; can customize via HFDD-PSCK program; production can be updated in batch only
DICTIONARY/3000	DBC	Password facility; security class code for any level, item to the whole D.B.

Available Data Dictionary/Directory System Packages

Owner/User Facility?	Exception/Error Reports?	Change Effect Reports?	Audit Trail Reports?	Management-Oriented Summaries/Custom Tailored Reports?
Yes	Yes	Yes	Yes	Yes
Yes	Yes	Yes	Yes	Yes
Yes	Yes	Yes	Yes	Yes
Yes	Yes	Yes	Yes	Yes
Yes	Yes	Yes	Yes	Yes
Yes	Yes	Yes	Yes	Yes
Yes	Yes	Yes	Yes	Yes

UCC Ten
Data Dictionary /
Manager *

UCC TEN OVERVIEW

UCC Ten Objectives

UCC TEN is a management and control facility designed primarily to meet the needs of IMS-DL/I data sharing operations. The Data Dictionary/Manager is an IMS application and operates under all releases of IMS and IMS/VS.

Specific objectives of the package are to:

1. Provide an automated mechanism through which standards for defining and using data can be established and enforced.
2. Improve productivity of the IMS-DL/I and OS operation.
3. Provide the comprehensive and usable definitions and cross-reference capabilities necessary to manage the many elements of an IMS-DL/I operation.

UCC TEN is a working data dictionary. Its design, scope and use are intended to compliment effective data base administration and management in the effort to realize the benefits available through positive data management practices. It is most effective in installations having this objective.

To accomplish its objectives, UCC TEN adheres to the principle that benefits realized through use of a dictionary are the result of:

1. The depth of data definitions supported.
2. Quality of the definitions in the dictionary.
3. The level of data usability provided.

With respect to definitional capability, UCC TEN supports all thirty-seven IMS-DL/I entities and the over three hundred attributes necessary to describe and establish entity relationships (i.e., interdependencies). This information is stored in the dictionary in an organized, structured, usable fashion. Through this capability, the entire IMS-DL/I environment is supported including: job streams, data bases, data set groups, segments, fields, programs, communication line groups, lines, physical and logical terminals, control units, pools/sub-pools and message format services.

To maintain integrity of definitions, UCC TEN performs extensive edits on input transactions to ensure that definitions conform to standards. Definitions which do not conform are simply not allowed in the dictionary. This accuracy checking very positively augments standards and control efforts and improves productivity by eliminating problems associated with "garbage in; garbage out" situations.

Through the courtesy of University Computing Company

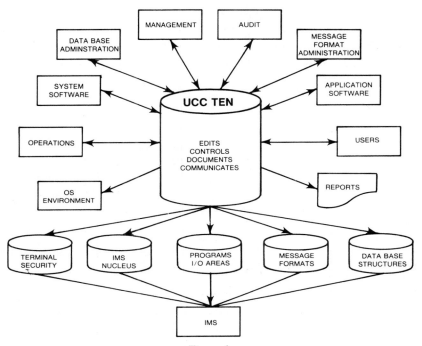

Figure 1.
UCC TEN Environment. (Courtesy University Computing Company.)

Usability of definitions stored in the dictionary is a bottom line measure of its capacity to improve overall productivity. The UCC TEN approach to providing this usability is twofold: informational use and physical use.

Informational use refers to the ability to query the dictionary to gain information important to a decision-making process. For example, the ability is provided to quickly and accurately determine through the dictionary which programs use which data bases, the length of a given segment and the number of programs which would be affected by a change to a record field.

This sort of information is in daily demand within a data sharing operation.

Physical use refers to the use of dictionary stored definitions to accomplish functions which would otherwise require manual effort.

Through the courtesy of University Computing Company

169

An example is the generation of IMS and Message Format Service control blocks and generation of program input/output areas. These tasks can consume human resources and result in errors and delays. Through UCC TEN, these and other tasks are accomplished accurately and automatically.

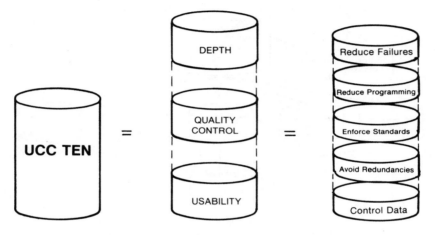

Figure 2.

UCC TEN objectives. (Courtesy University Computing Company.)

UCC TEN Components

UCC TEN consists of data bases, the UCC TEN inquiry (reporting) and updating facility and maintenance and service routines.

    In the data dictionary, production and development descriptions are maintained separately. This is commonly referred to as multiple dictionary sides and allows for manipulation (adding, revising, removing, etc.) of development data in the dictionary while leaving production definitions undisturbed and secure. There is a maximum of 255 dictionary sides in UCC TEN.

Through the courtesy of University Computing Company

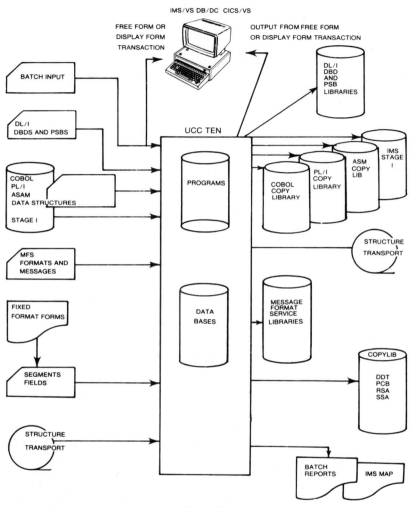

IMS/VS DB/DC CICS/VS

FREE FORM OR
DISPLAY FORM
TRANSACTION

OUTPUT FROM FREE FORM
OR DISPLAY FORM TRANSACTION

BATCH INPUT

DL/I
DBDS AND PSBS

COBOL
PL/I
ASAM
DATA STRUCTURES

STAGE I

MFS
FORMATS AND
MESSAGES

FIXED
FORMAT FORMS

SEGMENTS
FIELDS

STRUCTURE
TRANSPORT

UCC TEN

PROGRAMS

DATA
BASES

DL/I
DBD
AND
PSB
LIBRARIES

IMS
STAGE
I

ASM
COPY
LIB

PL/I
COPY
LIBRARY

COBOL
COPY
LIBRARY

STRUCTURE
TRANSPORT

MESSAGE
FORMAT
SERVICE
LIBRARIES

COPYLIB

DDT
PCB
RSA
SSA

BATCH
REPORTS

IMS MAP

Figure 3.

UCC TEN Components. (Courtesy University Computing Company.)

Information in the dictionary is added maintained and reported on through the UCC TEN Inquiry and Update facility. This
facility is operational online under IMS Data Communication (DC) and
under CiCS/VS. The facility is operational in batch mode through

Through the courtesy of University Computing Company

DATA BASE	SEGMENT	FIELD	APPLICATION
NAME	NAME	NAME	NAME
ATTRIBUTES	ATTRIBUTES	ATTRIBUTES	ATTRIBUTES
ACCESS METHOD ANCHOR POINTS RELATIVE BLOCK NUMBER RANDOMIZING MODULE RECORD TYPE LENGTH RECORD TYPE LOCATION TITLE ORGANIZATION TYPE DL/I PARAMETERS	MAXIMUM LENGTH MINIMUM LENGTH SEGMENT TYPE RECORD TYPE TITLE	TYPE LENGTH JUSTIFICATION LANGUAGE NAME OCCURS INDEXED	COMMENTS PROGRAMMER RESPONSIBILITY PHONE NUMBER TITLE
RELATIONSHIPS	RELATIONSHIPS	RELATIONSHIPS	RELATIONSHIPS
DATA BASE-DATA SET DATA BASE PSB	SEGMENT-FIELD SEGMENT-PSB SEGMENT-DATA SET	FIELD-SEGMENT FIELD-PROGRAM FIELD-LIST FIELD-ID FIELD-PSB	APPLICATION-JOB
JOB	PROGRAM	PSB	TEXT
NAME	NAME	NAME	NAME
ATTRIBUTES	ATTRIBUTES	ATTRIBUTES	ATTRIBUTES
COMMENTS TYPE TITLE	COMMENTS SOURCE LANGUAGE PROGRAMMER RESPONSIBLE PHONE NUMBER OVERLAY INFORMATION TITLE	MESSAGE CLASS LANGUAGE DL/I PARAMETERS OVERLAY INFORMATION TYPE TITLE	TYPE TEXT DESCRIPTION ELEMENT ASSOCIATION
RELATIONSHIPS	RELATIONSHIPS	RELATIONSHIPS	RELATIONSHIPS
JOB APPLICATION JOB PROGRAM	PROGRAM-JOB PROGRAM-PSB PROGRAM-FIELD PROGRAM-MODULE	PSB-LOGICAL TERMINAL PSB-SEGMENT	ALL ELEMENTS

Figure 4.

Typical Information Stored in UCC TEN. (Courtesy University Computing Company.)

Batch Message Processing (BMP) and normal IMS batch processing.

For on-line update, two input formats are provided, MENU and IMS transaction format. Both MENU (fill in the blank) and IMS transaction format may be used with Message Format Services (MFS) compatible terminals. Other terminals use only IMS transaction format for update functions.

Batch updating is accomplished through Batch Message Processing (concurrently with IMS on-line operation) or through normal IMS batch processing. Batch update input is in IMS transaction format.

Through the courtesy of University Computing Company

172

FORMAT	DEVICE	DIVISION	LINEGROUP
NAME	NAME	NAME	NAME
ATTRIBUTES	ATTRIBUTES	ATTRIBUTES	ATTRIBUTES
DL/I PARAMETERS TITLE	KEYBOARD TYPE PROGRAM FUNCTION KEYS UNIT TYPE RECORD LENGTH ALL MFS CHARACTERISTICS TITLE	FIELD EXIT ROUTINES SEGMENT EXIT ROUTINES DL/I PARAMETERS UNIT TYPE INPUT/OUTPUT TYPE	EDIT ROUTINES
RELATIONSHIPS	RELATIONSHIPS	RELATIONSHIPS	RELATIONSHIPS
FORMAT-DEVICE	DEVICE-FORMAT DEVICE-DIVISION	DIVISION-DEVICE DIVISION-DEVICE PAGE	LINE GROUP-LINE LINE GROUP-POOL
LINE	CONTROL UNIT	PHYSICAL TERMINAL	LOGICAL TERMINAL
NAME	NAME	NAME	NAME
ATTRIBUTES	ATTRIBUTES	ATTRIBUTES	ATTRIBUTES
BUFFER SIZE CONFIG NAME UNIT TYPE DL/I PARAMETERS TITLE	ADDRESS BUFFER SIZE PRINTER TYPE LOCATION TITLE DL/I PARAMETERS	TYPE ADDRESS BUFFER SIZE COMPONENT TYPE OUTPUT COMPONENTS DL/I PARAMETERS TRANSMISSION FEATURES UNIT TYPE LOCATION TITLE	OUTPUT COMPONENT EDIT MODULE MASTER TERMINAL DATA TITLE DL/I PARAMETERS
RELATIONSHIPS	RELATIONSHIPS	RELATIONSHIPS	RELATIONSHIPS
LINE-LINE GROUP LINE-CONTROL UNIT	CONTROL UNIT-LINE CONTROL UNIT-TERMINAL	TERMINAL-CONTROL UNIT TERMINAL-STATION TERMINAL-TERMINAL	TERMINAL-TERMINAL LOGICAL TERMINAL-POOL TERMINAL-TRANSACTION

Figure 4 (cont.)

Information in the dictionary is inquired or reported on through batch and on-line inquiry. This is accomplished through transactions which specify the information sought.

Inquiry and update are used to accomplish six dictionary functions: Data Entry, Data Structuring, Inquiry, Management, Service and Special Purpose. Figure 5 is a description of the operations associated with each function.

UCC TEN maintenance and service routines perform utility and housekeeping functions related to the dictionary and its use. For example, routines are provided to inspect and change data base records, create input to IMS security maintenance, compare current and previous system generation specifications, and delete and manipulate data structures.

Through the courtesy of University Computing Company

DATA ENTRY	
ADD	creates a new entity in the dictionary.
DELete	removes an entity from the dictionary.
REVise	modifies the attributes of an existing entity.

DATA STRUCTURING	
CONnect	establishes a relationship between two appropriate entities.
DISconnect	eliminates the relationship between two entities.
ALTer	eliminates an existing relationship and establishes a new relationship.

INQUIRY	
REPort	produces a formatted listing of an entity and may include its relationships.

MANAGEMENT	
SEQuence	renumbers entities of the dictionary that use sequence numbers.
REName	modifies the name by which an entity is known.
MOVe	causes an entity and its related entities to be made known to either the production or development side of the dictionary.
COPy	creates a new entity or structure identical in all respects except for name to an existing entity or structure.
DEQueue	removes a transaction from the queue data base.
DSTructure	removes all relationships from an entity structure. All entities will remain in the system.
DABsolute	removes all relationships from an entity structure and removes any entities that are not connected to other elements.

SERVICE	
GENerate	produces DBD or PSB source statements; MID, MOD, DIF, DOF source statements; I/O areas, SSAs, RSAs, PCBs in assembler, COBOL, or PL/I languages; GIS DDTs; and State I SYSGEN input from data stored in the dictionary.

SPECIAL	
EXECute	allows the user to execute specially written programs, particularly when accessing UCC TEN's data bases.

Figure 5

UCC TEN functions. (Courtesy University Computing Company.)

174

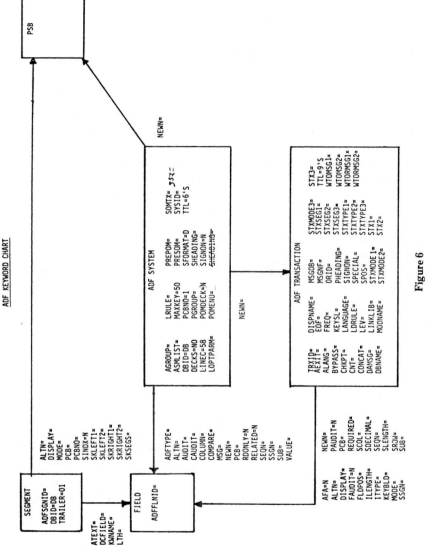

ADF KEYWORD CHART

Figure 6

ADF Relationships. (Courtesy University Computing Company.)

175

Additionally, maintenance and service routines produce reports for general use. A Glossary Report is provided for the UCC TEN Text Data Base; a Master Terminal Operator Report which shows the entire IMS network is provided to aid in troubleshooting activity; and various other reports are provided for status and control functions.

UCC TEN Features and Facilities

The following is a brief description of major UCC TEN features and facilities.

Single-Entry Definition: A troublesome and error generating aspect of IMS is the need to repetitively specify the same item of information in different formats to satisfy IMS input requirements. For a segment update, it may be necessary to specify a single item of information as many as eight times in different formats. For example, DBDs (Data Base Definitions) and PSBs (Program Specification Blocks) must be in macro format, the Program Control Block, Segment Search Argument and Input/Output areas could be COBOL, terminal security must be in macro format, and a cross-reference listing and other documentation in text format.

With UCC TEN, definitional information is specified once in the dictionary, in one format via one transaction. UCC TEN then cor-

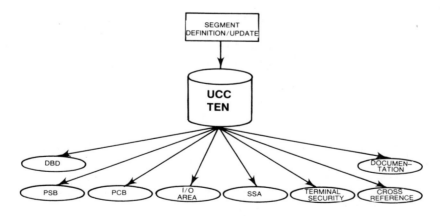

Figure 7.

UCC TEN Single Entry Definition/Update. (Courtesy University Computing Company.)

Through the courtesy of University Computing Company

rectly formats the item of information to meet input requirements for each area of use. If a change to an item of information is required, the change is made one time in the dictionary and all subsequent references to and generations of control blocks using that item of information reflect the change.

A facility unique to UCC TEN Single-Entry Definition provides ease of use and improves productivity because data entry time and effort are reduced. Mistakes are minimized through this feature since information is entered only once and then automatically used to satisfy all requirements associated with that item.

Editing: Use and enforcement of the standards is recognized as a most important activity in a data sharing operation. To assist in this critical area, UCC TEN performs automatic edits on all definitional data. As each input transaction is entered, it can be edited to determine if it conforms to standards and conventions. If it does not, it is rejected with a message specifying the reason for rejection.

The facility provides two advantages. First, standards are enforced at the time definitions are first entered in the dictionary. Nothing is defined which does not conform to standards. Secondly, problems, errors and omissions are detected, rejected and corrected during a clerical activity not during compile, test and production stages. This forced accuracy on the front end results in fewer compile, assembly and test errors.

Structure Independent Definitions: An important capability of UCC TEN is its usefulness during application design activity. Through Structure Independent Definition, UCC TEN provides for independent definition of application elements (i.e., descriptions of fields, segments, data set groups, etc.) as they are developed. Later, when relationships between these elements become known, definitions can be connected to make up the appropriate structures.

This allows design, development, definition and documentation to be accomplished in parallel, so that the "we'll do that later" approach to new application definition and documentation is avoided.

Language Independence: Definitions are entered into the Data Dictionary/Manager in language independent format through transactions which include the item of information being defined and its attributes. The dictionary then dynamically formats that information to meet language requirements. For example, program Input/Output areas can be automatically generated by UCC TEN in Assembler, COBOL and PL/I from a single set of information. IMS and

Message Format Services control blocks are produced in the same manner.

Language Independence addresses many of the time consuming, repetitive tasks associated with data definition by eliminating the clerical effort of re-coding and re-punching data simply to satisfy language and format requirements.

Automated Generation: Once required information is stored in the dictionary, control blocks are automatically generated by UCC TEN. The resultant blocks are directed to the appropriate IMS or copy library.

Definition Security: UCC TEN provides for specification of a password for any and all definitions in the dictionary. Using definition passwords, user security modules may be used to restrict or allow access to definitions at any level. Additionally, use of dictionary functions can be controlled. For example, a user may be given the ability to generate IMS control blocks but may be denied access to definitions at any level. Additionally, use of dictionary functions can be controlled. For example, a user may be given the ability to generate IMS control blocks but may be denied access to the update facility.

The dictionary maintains production and test (development) definitions separately. Updates to production definitions are controlled through special batch runs and through special keywords for on-line transactions thereby protecting the production definitions from haphazard updating.

Cross-Reference: Figure 8 shows how all thirty-seven IMS entities are utilized to determine the relationship between one entity and another. With this closed loop design and given one entity, all other related entities can be determined. The Cross-Reference facility enables a user to quickly and accurately answer questions such as, "what programs access a given segment," "what data bases are accessed by a program," and "what transactions can be submitted from a given terminal."

Using this facility, top-to-bottom, bottom-to-top, middle-to-top, and middle-to-bottom relationships can be quickly determined.

Deferred Transaction Processing: This feature allows dictionary inquiry and update transactions to be directed to the UCC TEN Queue data base on-line, and queued for batch processing against the dictionary at a later time. Through this feature, voluminous dictionary activity can be batched to gain processing efficiency.

Through the courtesy of University Computing Company

Keyword in Context/Keyword Out of Context: The keyword in context (KWIC) and keyword out of context (KWOC) facility functions dynamically within UCC TEN. As elements and attribute information are added or revised in the dictionary, user determined at-

UCC TEN

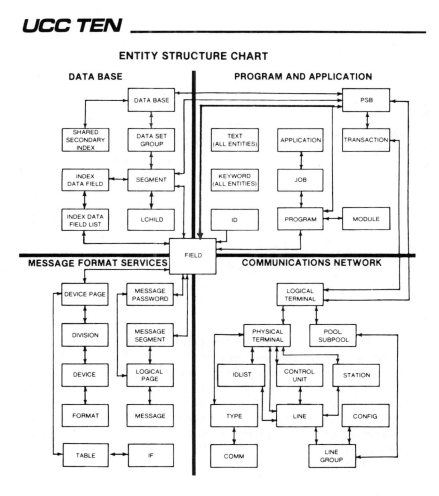

Figure 8.
UCC TEN Entity Structure Chart. (Courtesy University Computing Company.)

Through the courtesy of University Computing Company

the Keyword data base which relate the keywords to their references. The user may report on keywords (singularly or in combination) and obtain a list of all elements which use those keywords.

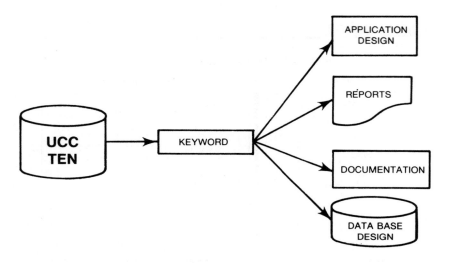

Figure 9.

UCC TEN Keyword Facility. (Courtesy University Computing Company.)

       The KWIC process may, at the user's option, occur for all element names and titles as well as COBOL and PL/I names. This also allows text areas to be a source for the keyword build process.

       The KWOC process is implemented at the user's option by establishing a standard area or areas of text which are to be scanned during the keyword build process. These areas of the text can contain keywords out of context which have been placed there by the user. The keyword report facility can subsequently be used to obtain meaningful reference lists.

       Documentation/Text: Textual documentation, as well as structure and entities documentation, is a very necessary part of any application. UCC TEN provides for collection of textual documentation for each of the entities in the dictionary. When these entities are

Through the courtesy of University Computing Company

structured (connected) to form a composite group definition, the text information can be extracted with the structure definition to form a complete documentation package. This is especially important in the case of field entities where one field may be structured to one or more segments, in one or more data bases.

Text information can be supplied for each entity in one or more of three separate categories. These categories are: (1) general description, (2) edit requirements, and (3) source/responsibility.

General description information should always be input for each entity to provide a complete definition. The remaining two areas

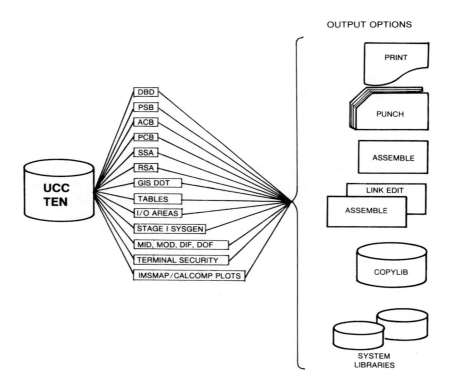

Figure 10.

UCC TEN Automatically Generates Control Blocks. (Courtesy University Computing Company.)

Through the courtesy of University Computing Company

should be used as required. An example would be the definition of a field. General description data could be used to explain the function of the field. If editing is required, the edit requirements can be listed in this section. When a particular organization or person is responsible for inputting the field, name, organization, and/or input sources can be documented in that category.

Reporting: One key to usefulness is the ease with which information can be extracted from the dictionary and how effective that information is in meeting the user needs. With UCC TEN, both batch and on-line reports are provided.

With UCC TENs "selective level" reporting, levels of information may be selected and reported on.

For example, for a report on a data base, one option is to report only the data base name and its attributes. Another option is to report the data base, the data set group, and even each segment and field connected to that data base.

Fixed Format Input: Several forms have been designed to aid the user when inputting large volumes of certain dictionary transactions. These fixed format forms and the associated UCC TEN routines provide the user an easier method to code, keypunch and input (to a UCC TEN batch run) large volumes of field adds, segment-to-field connects and device page-to-field connects. Error checking is performed on the field values of the input transactions. The user is given the option of a preliminary run to indicate errors before placing input transactions into the dictionary. This technique is especially helpful for I/O area and device page definitions since changes can be made to input prior to affecting UCC TEN data bases.

An added feature of fixed format routines is the ability to produce a special report for screen format data. As the input is scanned, all device page-to-field connections are processed. The result is a printout of each physical page in screen image format. Being able to review this image and correct errors provides rapid and accurate development of MFS formats.

Structure Transport: UCC TEN provides a structure transport facility which allows dictionary structures to be moved between physically separate dictionaries. The unload function of the structure transport facility creates a sequential output file consisting of records from the unloaded structure. The load function uses the file created by the unload function to reconstruct the structure in the receiving

Through the courtesy of University Computing Company

dictionary. Elements are not deleted by the transport function. Four types of structures can be extracted: data base structures, application structures, message structures and format structures.

IMS System Generation Comparison: Traditionally, IMS system generations are performed when the current IMS system requires a change. These changes may be adding a new data base definition (DBD), deleting a program specification block (PSB), etc.

The UCC TEN IMS system generation comparison facility provides for SYSGEN data to be 'saved' after an IMS system generation is completed. This data can then be automatically compared with the current SYSGEN data in the UCC TEN data bases when a new SYSGEN is produced. Messages indicating added or dropped data are produced in the comparison thus indicating the data that has changed since the previous IMS system generation.

IMS Security Maintenance Input: UCC TEN creates input to the IMS security maintenance utility. In addition to this input, a security maintenance matrix printout is available. This matrix printout aids both the IMS system programmer and the IMS master terminal operator in identifying transaction-to-terminal relationship.

Master Terminal Operator Report: The terminal report provides the master terminal operator complete documentation for the data communication facility (on-line IMS).

Reports provided show the following relations:

1. line group-line-physical terminal-logical terminal
2. transaction-program-data base

These reports can be time saving in a problem situation.

Entering Information in the Dictionary

UCC TEN facilities enable users to define and maintain data relating to the IMS data base applications, the IMS data communications environment, or application systems using standard O/S file organization. UCC TEN allows transactions to be entered and updates to be made in four different modes. This allows the user to tailor UCC TEN to the specific operational environment.

The first method of operation is inputting and updating on-line using formatted 3270's or unformatted terminals. The second method of input is on-line using formatted 3270's or unformatted terminals and updating in batch (deferred transaction processing). The third method of input and updating is in the batch message processing mode. The fourth method of input is the batch mode.

All structures in UCC TEN may be started at any element level (i.e. top-to-bottom, bottom-to-top, etc.). The top-to-bottom method is used to construct an IMS data base description (DBD). The first UCC TEN formatted screen to be displayed is the MENU screen in Figure 11.

```
UCC TEN
                                       UCC  TEN
                               DATA  DICTIONARY/MANAGER

   FUNCTIONS         ELEMENT #1          ELEMENT #2          PSWD

   FUNCTIONS..  ADD ALT CON COP DEL DEQ DIS EXEC GEN HELP MASS REN REP REV

      STRUCTURE                        ELEMENTS
   DATABASE/FILE......  DBN, DSN, SGN, FLN, ALNM, LCN, XDF, LIST (DBD, DDT, I/O)
   APPLICATION........  APN, JBN, PGN, MDN, PSB, FLN, ITRN, OTRN, LTN
   FORMAT.............  FMT, FDEV, FDIV, FDPG, TBN, IFN, FLN
   MESSAGE............  MSGN, MLPN, MSEG, MPSW, FLN
   COMMUNICATIONS.....  COMN, LGN, PLN, CFN, LNAD, IDLN, CUN, STN, LTN, PTN, TYPN
   DOCUMENTATION......  KW, TXN

         ---------------  PROGRAM FUNCTION KEYS - FORMAT SELECTION  ---------------
   PFK01 HELP - HELP RETURN   PFK02 MENU                PFK03 REPORT
   PFK04 GEN I/O              PFK05 GEN PSB             PFK06 FLN ADD
   PFK07 FLN/SGN CONNECT      PFK07 FLN/FDPG CONNECT    PFK09 FLN/MSEG CONNECT
   PFK10 DSN/SGN CONNECT      PFK11 PSB/SGN CONNECT

   *HELP FUNCTION USED WITH ELEMENTS DBN, DSN, SGN, FLN, ALNM, LCN, XDF, LIST
```

Figure 11.
UCC TEN MENU. (Courtesy University Computing Company.)

The terminal operator may add a data base by entering ADD and DBD in the FUNCTION and ELEMENT fields on the MENU screen. If password security is being used, the operator will also enter an assigned security code in the PASSWORD field.

Figure 12 illustrates the UCC TEN formatted screen through which a data base element will be entered in the dictionary.

```
                                  UCC  TEN
                       DATA  DICTIONARY/MANAGER

      ADD    MSGID  99999  OLC  SYSPRINT  IPN  UNKNOWN    QUE  N  PSWD
             DBN           AMET      DL/I     TTL
               SYSG        VSAM      DOS      PROT    PASS   RES
      RMOD     APTS                  MRBN        BYTE
               RTLN        RTLO
             NEXT  1B00
```

Figure 12.
Add Data Base. (Courtesy University Computing Company.)

The only required entry would be the data base name (DBN). UCC TEN will automatically assume all standard IMS defaults. UCC TEN contains 'HELP' screens to aid the user in using the on-line facility. The 'HELP' function eliminates the need for any reference material as information is readily available by using a specified program function key. Figure 13 is an example of 'HELP' screens for the data base add function.

Through the courtesy of University Computing Company

```
        UCC TEN DATA DICTIONARY/MANAGER UCC TEN
            NON IMS DATA BASE HELP SCREEN DEFAULT

  DBN=XXXXXXXX                            FILE NAME   NONE


  AMET=XX                                 ACCESS METHOD      NONE
        UCC TEN DATA DICTIONARY/MANAGER UCC TEN
            IMS DATA BASE HELP SCREEN DEFAULT

    THE FOLLOWING KEYWORDS APPLY ONLY IF AMET-HD (HDAM)
        UCC TEN DATA DICTIONARY/MANAGER UCC TEN
            IMS DATA BASE HELP SCREEN DEFAULT

  VSAM=X   IS THIS DATA BASE VSAM OR ISAM/OSAM?        Y
           Y - YES, VSAM   N - NO,ISAM/OSAM



        UCC TEN DATA DICTIONARY/MANAGER UCC TEN
            IMS DATA BASE HELP SCREEN DEFAULT

  FUNCTION          ELEMENT #1          ELEMENT #2         PSWD

  DBN=XXXXXXXX                               DATA BASE NAME      NONE

  AMET=XX ACCESS METHOD                           HI

          DE - DEDB     HI - HISAM    IN - INDEX     SI - SHISAM
          GS - GSAM     HS - HSAM     LO - LOGICAL   SS - SHSAM
          HD - HDAM     ID - HIDAM    MS - MSDB

  DL/I=X   IS THIS A DL/I DATA BASE?                  Y
           Y - YES       N - NO


  TTL=XXXXXXXXXXXXXXXXXXXXXXXXXXXXXX      TITLE      30 B'S

  SYSG=X   IS THIS DATA BASE TO BE INCLUDED IN IMS STAGE-1 SYSGEN?    N
           Y - YES       N - NO


           HIT KEY PA1 FOR NEXT PAGE OF KEYWORDS
```

Figure 13.

UCC TEN HELP Screen. (Courtesy University Computing Company.)

186

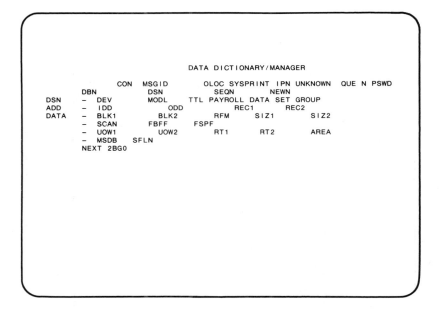

```
                    DATA DICTIONARY/MANAGER

                 CON   MSGID          OLOC SYSPRINT IPN UNKNOWN    QUE N PSWD
           DBN                DSN         SEQN          NEWN
  DSN      -   DEV          MODL     TTL PAYROLL DATA SET GROUP
  ADD      -   IDD               ODD                REC1          REC2
  DATA     -   BLK1           BLK2         RFM       SIZ1          SIZ2
           -   SCAN       FBFF      FSPF
           -   UOW1           UOW2         RT1       RT2           AREA
           -   MSDB    SFLN
           NEXT 2BG0
```

Figure 14.

Data Base/Data Set Group Connect. (Courtesy University Computing Company.)

Continuing in the top-to-bottom method of creating the data base structure, the next element to be created is the data set group. Figure 14 illustrates the UCC TEN 3270 formatted screen in which the data set group will be entered into the system. In order to establish the relationship between the data base and the data set group, a connect function will be performed.

The segment is the next element to be defined to the system. With UCC TEN, any element may be added and a relationship established with one transaction. For example, a segment can be added and connected to the data set group in a single transaction. Figure 15 illustrates the 3270 formatted screen through which this is accomplished.

To complete the data base structure, field elements are connected to the segment, as shown in Figure 16.

tributes are scanned and "keywords" extracted for future reference. The scan process, called keyword build, causes entries to be made in

Through the courtesy of University Computing Company

187

UCC TEN
DATA DICTIONARY/MANAGER

```
                    CON  MSGID        OLOC SYSPRINT IPN UNKNOWN QUE N PSWD
DSN/SGN             DSN      -   LEV       SGN          SEQN         ALTN
CONNECT                                -   PPRN PPPT  LPRN  LPPT  NEWN
DATA    -   SSG1             SDK1       FREQ           PTRS  RULE  LDB
        -   SSG2             SDK2       SDB1
        -   CRTN             CPDK       SDB2
        -   SEQ                         INIT
SGN     -   TYPE   TTL
ADD     -   MAXB   MINB
DATA    -   RTYP
            NEXT 2GS0
```

Figure 15.

Data Set Group/Segment Connect. (Courtesy University Computing Company.)

UCC TEN
DATA DICTIONARY/MANAGER

```
                 CON  MSGID      OLOC         IPN UNKNOWN QUE N PSWD
                       SGN            FLN DEFNO    SEQN

SGN/FLN  –    SEQ   SNML   STRT
CONNECT  –    RDN   RFLG   GRP   OCCR  OCRD      DEFNO 000
DATA     –    OCRM  SKEY   SUFX  ILST  KLST
              VALU
FLN      –    ID    PIC    TYPE  USAG  JUST      EDWD
ADD      –    TTL
DATA     –    CBLN/PLIN
              UAB1   UAB2   ALL 1

              NEXT 2FS0
```

Figure 16.

Segment/Field Connect. (Courtesy University Computing Company.)

189

BIBLIOGRAPHY

ARDEN, BRUCE W., ed. "Interactive Computer Systems," *IEEE Proc.,* vol. 63, no. 6 (June 1975), pp. 833-979.

AUERBACH, *Auerbach Guide to Data Base Management.* Pennsauken, NJ: Auerbach Publishers. p. 209.

BAYER, RUDOLF, "Storage Characteristics and Methods for Searching and Addressing," *Information Processing-74,* North-Holland.

BJORK, LAWRENCE A., Jr., "Generalized Audit Trail Requirements and Concepts for Data Base Applications," *IBM Systems, J.,* vol. 14, no. 3 (1975).

BOOTH, A.D., and J.T. COLIN, "On the Efficiency of a New Method of Dictionary Construction," *Information and Control,* vol. 3, no. 4 (Dec. 1960), pp. 327-34.

BOOTH, GRAYCE M., *Functional Analysis of Information Processing.* New York: John Wiley, 1973.

BRITISH COMPUTER SOCIETY, "Draft Data Dictionary Systems Working Party Report," *Data Base (ACM SIGBDP)*, vol. 9, no. 2 (Fall 1977).

BROWNE, PETER S., "Computer Security—A Survey," *Data Base (ACM SIGBDP)*, vol. 4, no. 3 (Fall 1972).

CAGAN, CARL, *Data Management Systems.* Melville Publishers, 1973.

CANNING, RICHARD G., *EDP Analyzer,* Vista, CA: Canning Publications, monthly newsletter since 1964.

CANNING, RICHARD G., "Installing a Data Dictionary," *EDP Analyzer,* vol. 16, no. 1 (Jan. 1978).

CARLSON, ERIC D., "Evaluating the Impact of Information Systems," *Management Datamatics* (IAG, Amsterdam), vol. 3, no. 2 (1974).

DONOVAN, JOHN J., "Database System Approach to Management Decision Support," *TODS,* vol. 1, no. 4 (Dec. 1976).

EVEREST, GORDON C., "The Objective of Data Base Management," *Proc. 4th International Symposium on Computer & Information Sciences,* Plenum Press, 1974.

FEDERAL INFORMATION PROCESSING STANDARDS TASK GROUP 17, *A Survey of Eleven Government Developed Data Element Dictionary/Directory Systems,* NBS Special Publication 500-16, US Dept. of Commerce, National Bureau of Standards, US Government Printing Office, Aug. 1977.

FRAILEY, DENNIS J., "A Practical Approach to Managing Resources and Avoiding Deadlock," *CACM,* vol. 16, no. 5 (May 1973).

FRIEDMAN, THEODORE D., "The Authorization Problem in Shared Files," *IBM System Journal,* vol. 9, no. 4 (1970).

GIRDANSKY, M.B., "Data Privacy, Cryptology and the Computer at IBM Research," *Computers and Automation,* (April 1972).

GUTHRIE, R.D., "A Data Dictionary Approach to MIS," *Datamation,* (April 1973), pp. 91-2.

HELLERMAN, HERBER and THOMAS F. CONROY, *Computer Systems Performance.* New York: McGraw-Hill, 1975.

HICKS, M., "Data Dictionary Can Impact Every Department," *Computer World,* (Dec. 10, 1979), p. 34.

HOFFMAN, LANCE J., *Modern Methods for Computer Security and Privacy.* Englewood Cliffs, NJ: Prentice-Hall, 1977.

IBM G320-1370-1376, Data Security and Data Processing, vols. 1-6, *IBM DPD,* 1974.

INF, Information Systems, Pergamon Press, journal since 1974.

KING, W.F., ed., International Conference on Management of Data (Proc. 1975 SIGMOD Conf.), *ACM*, 1975.

LEONG-HONG, B. and B. MARRON, Technical Profile of Seven Data Element Dictionary/Directory Systems, NBS Special Pub. 500-3, US Dept. of Commerce, National Bureau of Standards, US Government Printing Office, Feb. 1977.

LUCAS, HENRY C., Jr., *Why Information Systems Fail.* New York: Columbia University Press, 1975.

MARTIN, JAMES, *Computer Data-Base Organization* (2nd ed.), Englewood Cliffs, NJ: Prentice-Hall, 1977.

McEWEN, HAZEL E., ed. Management of Data Elements in Information Processing, US Dept. of Commerce, COM 74-10700, NTIS, Springfield, VA, April 1974.

MEALY, GEORGE H., "Another Look at Data," *Proc. 1967 FJCC, AFIPS,* vol. 31.

ROSS, RONALD G., "Data Dictionary System Needs Its Own Definition," *Computer World,* (Oct. 31, 1977), pp. S/3-S/10.

RUSTIN, RANDALL, ed. Data Description, Access, and Control (Proc. 1974 SIGFIDET Conf.), *ACM* (1974).

SCHREIBER, FABIO A. and G. MARTELLA, "Creating a Conceptual Model of a Data Dictionary for Distributed Data Bases," *Data Base, ACM, (SIGBDP),* vol. 11, no. 1 (Summer 1979).

SCHUSSEL, GEORGE, "The Role of the Data Dictionary," *Datamation* (June 1977).

SCHWARTZ, EUGENE S., "A Dictionary for Minimum Redundancy Encoding," *JACM,* vol. 10, no. 4 (Oct. 1963).

SENKO, MICHAEL E., "Information Systems—Records, Relations, Sets, Entities, and Things," *Information Systems,* vol. 1, no. 1, Pergamon Press (Jan. 1975).

STRNAD, ALOIS L., "The Relational Approach to the Management of Data Bases," *Information Processing-71,* North-Holland.

THOMAS, DAVID, "Data Management Eased With Dictionary Use," *Computer World* (Dec. 12, 1977), pp. 27-28.

UHROWCZIK, P.P., "Data Dictionary/Directories," *IBM System Journal,* vol. 12, no. 4 (Dec. 1973).

WIEDERHOLD, GIO, *Database Design.* New York: McGraw-Hill, 1977.

INDEX

A

Abbreviations, standard,
    56, 64-65
Accounting Subsystem, 15
Acronyms, standard,
    56, 64-65
Analysis phase, 71-75, 105-6
Andersen, Arthur, & Co.,
    156
Application-specification
    tables, 52
Auditors, 27

Audit-trail reports, 127, 153
Average data dictionary
    system, 49-51

B

"Base data" data
    elements, 56, 65, 73
Basic data dictionary
    system, 48-49
Batch processing, 152,
    172-73